**Anchor** THE NEW ANCHOR BOOK OF

Pulled Thread

EMBROIDERY STITCHES

THE NEW ANCHOR BOOK OF

Pulled Thread

EMBROIDERY STITCHES

David and Charles

About the Embroidery Designer

The designs in this book were created by Christine Wilkins. Christine runs Alchemy Stitchcraft, a needlecraft company that produces a large range of kits. She regularly contributes to needlecraft magazines.

A DAVID & CHARLES BOOK

David & Charles is a subsidiary of F + W (UK) Ltd.,
an F + W Publications Inc. company

Published in association with
COATS CRAFTS UK

First published in the UK in 1987
as *The Anchor Book of Counted Thread Embroidery Stitches*
Revised edition published 1997
This edition published 2005

Distributed in North America
by F + W Publications, Inc.
4700 East Galbraith Road
Cincinnati, OH 45236
1-800-289-0963

A catalogue record for this book is available from the British Library.

ISBN 0 7153 1916 7

Printed in Singapore by KHL Printing Co Pte Ltd.
for David & Charles
Brunel House   Newton Abbot   Devon

Embroidery designs and project makes by Christine Wilkins
Photography by Karl Adamson, Kim Sayer and Julien Busselle
Text originally compiled by Eve Harlow and revised for this edition by Betsy Hosegood

Executive Editor   Cheryl Brown
Desk Editor   Ame Verso
Art Editor   Prudence Rogers
Designer   Sarah Underhill
Production Controller   Jennifer Campbell

Visit our website at www.davidandcharles.co.uk

David & Charles books are available from all good bookshops; alternatively you can contact our Orderline on (0)1626 334555 or write to us at FREEPOST EX2 110, David & Charles Direct, Newton Abbot, TQ12 4ZZ (no stamp required UK mainland).

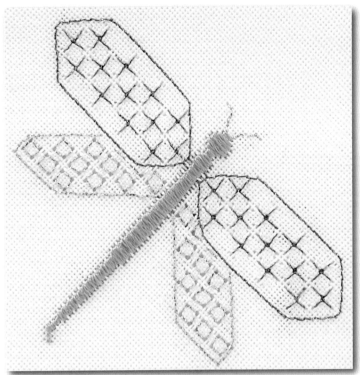

Contents

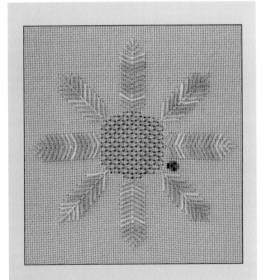

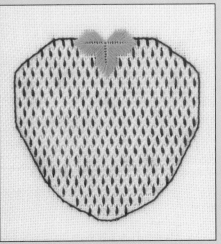

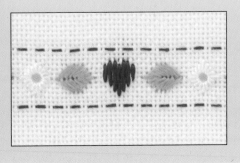

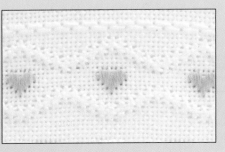

Introduction

Pulled thread work is a form of counted thread embroidery with a difference. What makes it special is that instead of looking at the stitches, your eyes are drawn to the pattern of the fabric. This is because the technique involves pulling the embroidery thread so tight that it distorts the threads of the fabric, drawing them into a decorative pattern of holes.

Pulled thread work falls into a category known as whitework because it was traditionally carried out on white fabric in white thread. Hardanger embroidery and drawn thread embroidery also fall into this category, but with these two styles the fabric is cut to create lacy fabrics whereas pulled work does not require any cutting and therefore the fabric remains much stronger.

The origins of pulled thread work are distant and exotic. If you wear a piece of pulled thread work you will be following in the footsteps of Cleopatra who wore it in around 50BC and in the centuries that followed we know that it was worked in India, Peru and the Middle East. In Europe it reached its heights in the 1800s, first in Germany and Denmark, then spreading to the rest of Europe and America. At the time it was designed to mimic expensive lace, and the finest pieces were worked in complicated designs using many different stitches.

In the 18th century pulled thread work was often stitched on very fine fabrics with thread counts of up to 100 to the inch. However, there was another strand of more robust pulled thread work going on among the 'peasant' classes, such as those in Greece and Turkey, and in some regions it was worked in a colour that contrasted with the cloth. Today's embroiderers can draw what they like from these origins, but fabrics of about 28 threads to the inch are perhaps the most popular, enabling us to create beautiful designs in a reasonable time span.

Working the Embroidery

Pulled thread embroidery is actually extremely simple compared with many other types of embroidery and most stitches or fillings are based on straight or satin stitches.

You'll find a wide selection of stitches on pages 22–50. These are listed alphabetically so they are easy to find. Alongside each stitch is an embroidered sample so you can see the finished result, but the steps for each stitch are shown as diagrams, which are usually clearer and easier to follow than stitched samples. There are also 16 pulled thread designs, such as the Beehive below left and on page 51, that display each stitch in use and these are referenced in the individual stitch introductions.

Although pulled thread embroidery can be used on its own, it is often combined with other embroidery stitches. In order to enable you to complete all the designs in this book and to work pieces of your own, instructions are given for a good range of additional stitches that combine well with pulled thread work and these can be found in the section on pages 55–63.

No book on pulled thread work would be complete without a sampler (see opposite), the traditional means of trying out new stitches, and you'll find details for working this one on pages 52–53 along with a complete alphabet on page 54 to enable you to include your own wording. Feel free to work your favourite stitches on any areas of the design and choose your own colours, if desired, to suit your taste or that of the recipient.

■ *Early European samplers were a means by which the embroiderer could store stitches she had learnt from books or seen in other people's embroideries. Later samplers often included alphabets or worthy sayings, and it is out of this genre that the commemorative sampler (opposite) was born. This one marks a wedding, but you could easily adapt it to celebrate a birth.*

Materials and Equipment

Pulled thread work requires minimal materials. You will need the fabric, thread in one or more colours, needles, scissors and a frame for mounting the fabric while it is being worked. The only additional items you may need are for finishing your piece, and these depend on how you plan to display your work (see pages 14–15).

Fabric

When choosing a fabric, look for something that is fairly loose, not tightly woven, otherwise you won't be able to pull the fabric into the required design. If necessary, push a tapestry needle between the threads on a corner of the fabric and see if the threads move apart quite easily. For a framed piece something like Anchor Jobelan (see below) is ideal.

Linen is the traditional favourite for all counted thread work and many embroiderers feel that the needle slides between the threads more smoothly than with any other fabric. It is available in many weights and thread counts from 14 to 32 to the inch. White, natural and ecru are the most commonly available colours but you can find it in other colours too.

Cotton is also traditional and comes in thread counts of up to 28 to the inch, which is suitable for all but the very finest of pulled thread work. Like linen, it is available in a number of colours as well as neutrals such as cream.

Hardanger in a fine count such as 22 threads to the inch can be used for pulled thread work but the lower counts have a tendency to look very chunky and naïve. You may, however, find this a good fabric to practice on.

Anchor Jobelan is used for all the designs in this book. It is a 28-count fabric, making it fine enough for quite detailed work and it is made from a practical blend of cotton and Modal. The texture of this fabric is very smooth and even and the threads are bold enough for you to count quite easily. It comes in 15 subtle colours so you should be able to find a colour to suit your design.

Evenweave fabric made in mixed fibres usually combines the look of linen or cotton with the practicalities of other fibres. Anchor's evenweave fabric is made from a blend of linen, cotton and Modal. It has a slubbed texture, like pure linen, and comes in seven pastel hues and white.

Embroidery Threads

Thread for pulled work must be strong because you have to pull quite hard on it. There is nothing worse than it snapping off in the middle of a long row of stitching. Traditionally it should also be the same thickness as the fabric threads.

If you wish to reproduce the style of 18th and 19th century European pulled thread work choose a thread that matches the fabric or is just a shade darker. Pearl cotton is a good choice, being strong and easy to work with, with a subtle sheen that doesn't call attention away from the pattern of holes in the fabric. If you prefer the bolder effects or wish

> ### ■ Thread Thickness
> The best way of checking that your thread is the right thickness is to pull off a thread from the edge of the fabric and lay it next to your proposed sewing thread. Ideally they should be roughly the same thickness.

If you prefer bolder effects or wish to take advantage of the array of threads available today then there is no reason why you shouldn't experiment.

Anchor Pearl Cotton is a 2-ply, loosely cabled thread with a soft sheen that is available in several thicknesses – Anchor Pearl Cotton comes in sizes 3, 5, 8 and 12 with No. 12 being the finest. It is excellent for pulled thread work, being strong enough to withstand the tension needed. You can use any thickness for pulled thread work but ideally match the thickness to that of the fabric threads (see the tip, left).

Anchor Coton à Broder is a 3-ply mercerized cotton with a lustrous finish. It is a popular choice for whitework, including pulled thread work, being fine enough to work quite intricate designs. Ticket 16 is the most popular thickness and comes in a range of colours.

Anchor Stranded Cotton has an attractive soft sheen finish. Its six strands can be worked together or separated into groups of three, two or even one strand for finer work. Most of the designs in this book that use stranded cotton are stitched with two strands, although some require only one strand in which case this is specified. In general, however, you should use at least two strands because one strand is not always sufficient for stitches that require a lot of tension on the thread. There are 472 colours in the Anchor range, including muliticolors.

Anchor Marlitt thread is a 4-ply thread made from viscose/rayon that has a very high sheen and comes in 90 rich colours. Like coton à broder it is suitable for most styles of pulled thread work but it makes more of a statement than the cotton thread. Marlitt thread is not quite as fine as stranded cotton, so when it is used for the designs in this book only one strand is needed. However, two strands are used for satin stitch to give better coverage. Marlitt is used for the Dragonfly (page 43) and several other designs in this book.

Coats Ophir is a synthetic metallic thread made from viscose and polyester. It cannot be washed in hot water so it isn't suitable for heavily used items. It is very fine for delicate effects and available in gold or silver. It is used in Festive Lace (page 29).

Coats Reflecta is a glittery thread made from polyester and available in nine colours. It is used in Champagne Celebration (page 35) and on the Dragonfly (page 43) where it captures the shimmer of the insect's wings. Like Ophir thread it cannot be divided into strands.

Linen thread is available only in a few colours including black, white and ecru. Use it if you are planning a traditional design and wish to be as authentic as possible.

If you enjoy experimentation you may wish to try some of the other threads and cottons available. Very fine crochet or tatting cotton could work well for traditional pieces or you might try some of the more exotic metallics. However, some of these, especially the more expensive varieties, can be fragile and are really only suitable for laid work; you will need a fairly strong thread for pulled thread work.

Hoops and Frames

Pulled thread work involves deliberately distorting the fabric, but this is a controlled distortion and in order to prevent the fabric from completely pulling out of shape you

should always mount your work in a frame or hoop. These also keep your work flat for easier thread counting. Choose a size that gives you room to work the design easily and feels comfortable in your hands. A hoop 20 or 25cm (8 or 10in) across should suit most of the designs in this book but if you are happier using one of the other styles of frames then by all means do.

A **wooden embroiderer's hoop**, also known as a tambour frame, is the most popular choice. It has two rings, one inside the other, and works by trapping the fabric between them, using an adjustable screw to tighten the tension on the outer ring. It is quick to fit and easy to use. To hold the fabric more securely and help prevent the hoop from leaving marks, many embroiderers bind the inner hoop with bias cotton tape. Even if you do this, it is advisable to remove your work after each stitching session. If left in the hoop for too long the tension on the fabric can lead to distortions around the frame position.

A **stretcher frame** is made from four wooden slats joined together to form a square or rectangle. The fabric can be stapled on to it to hold it taut. The disadvantage of this type of frame is that it is not easy to re-adjust the tension of the fabric if it begins to slacken as work progresses. However, once properly fitted, you can leave the fabric in place until it is finished.

An **upholstered frame** is like a stretcher frame except that it is more solid and has been covered with padding and fabric. The working fabric is simply pinned on to the frame and can be moved across as work progresses or if the tension needs adjustment.

A **rotating hand frame** is suitable for large designs and you won't need one for the projects in this book. It is a rectangular frame with a roller at top and bottom. The fabric is stitched to cotton tape on each of the rollers, with the excess fabric rolled around them neatly until the fabric is taught. The sides of the fabric can then be laced to the sides of the frame. The idea is that as the design progresses the fabric can be rolled on to expose a new area of fabric, ready to work. This has the advantage that the fabric on the rollers is kept clean and neatly out of the way.

Needles

Use a tapestry needle, which has a blunt point so that it can pass easily between the fabric threads. Choose a needle with a hole large enough for the thread to slide through without fraying but still fine enough to fit easily through the fabric. Size 24 or 26 should be sufficient for most work.

Scissors

You'll need a pair of dressmakers' scissors (shears) to cut the fabric to shape and a pair of small, fine-pointed scissors to trim off the ends of the embroidery threads close to the work.

Additional Equipment

Pulled thread work demands precision when counting threads and for this you will need good lighting, ideally in the form of a bright floor or table lamp. For detailed work you may like to consider a magnifying glass. You will need one that hangs around the neck or attaches to your glasses, keeping your hands free.

> ### ■ Comfort in Mind
> *Always make sure that your design fits comfortably inside the hoop or frame so that the edges don't restrict your embroidery hand. If using a hoop never allow the embroidery to become trapped between the two hoops.*

Getting Started

Here are the basics to get you started with pulled thread techniques. If you have already tried other forms of embroidery some of it may be familiar to you, but it is a good idea to read through this information anyway because there are items here that are specific to pulled thread work.

Working from a Chart

Pulled thread work designs are stitched from charts, as are all other counted thread work patterns. Once you understand the principles of doing this you'll find it really easy, and there is less room for confusion than when following written instructions.

You may already be familiar with the charts for cross stitch in which one square on the chart represents an intersection of crossing fabric threads, or if the fabric is fine, an intersection of two pairs of crossing fabric threads. Some of the charts in this book work on the same principle, especially when they also involve cross stitch. In the remaining charts the lines on the grid represent the fabric threads to help you visualize the stitching process. In each case there is a note in the text beside the chart pointing out how it works.

Preparing the Fabric

To work each design you will need a piece of suitable fabric larger than your chosen motif and also large enough to fit comfortably in your hoop or frame (see the previous page). Linen fabrics and some of the other loose-weave fabrics suitable for pulled work are especially prone to fraying so it is a good idea to secure the edges of your fabric as soon as you have cut it to size by oversewing, working machine zigzag around the edges or applying masking tape around all the sides.

Next mark the centre of your fabric so that you can position the design centrally on it. To do this fold the fabric along the length, make a light crease along the fold, open it back out and tack (baste) along the crease line. Repeat to fold and tack the fabric centrally along the width. The two lines of tacking stitches cross in the centre of the fabric. Most charts indicate the centre lines with black arrows at the edges. Unless otherwise instructed, start stitching in the centre of the design, matching the centre lines of your chart with the tacking lines on your fabric.

Order of Working

Most patterns will advise you on the order of working, but it is usual with pulled thread work to stitch the outline of each area before the filling. Once the outline is in place it is clear where you need to work the filling and you will have a handy place to secure the end of your working thread. Simply weave the new thread through the back of the outline stitches, beginning with a back stitch to secure it.

Starting and Finishing

Securing thread ends in pulled thread embroidery needs to be done with care because of the open pattern created by the pulled threads. For the same reason it is important not to run threads from one area of the design to another. Ideally finish the thread in one area and then begin afresh in the next. If you must run the thread across the back, take a small stitch through the fabric every 5mm (¼in) or so to secure it.

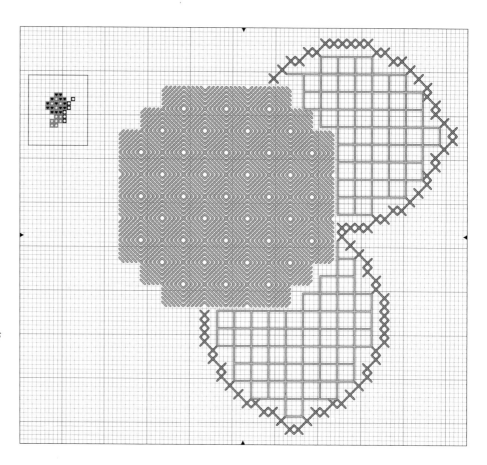

■ *Here is a typical example of a chart in this book, which is used for the Blue Hydrangea design on page 31. Each square on the chart represents one pair of intersecting fabric threads. The black arrows at the sides mark the centre of the design to help you locate it on the fabric. Start stitching at the centre.*

Waste knot There are several ways of starting a new thread, but one of the simplest is the waste knot (away waste knot) method. Start by making a large knot in the end of the thread and insert the needle from the right side of the fabric about 10cm (4in) away from your first stitch in an area that will be worked later. Bring your needle out in the required place and begin stitching. When you finish the length of thread secure the end (see right). Clip off your knot and pull the thread through to the wrong side of the fabric. Thread on your needle and weave the thread end through the back of the stitches.

In-line method Start your stitching leaving a 5–8cm (2–3in) length behind the fabric. Work your stitches, aligning the thread end underneath so that it is caught as you work. This saves time in the long run but can be fiddly to start off with.

Darning Once some of the stitching has been worked you can begin a new thread by weaving it through the back of the existing stitches. If desired, you can start with a back stitch for added security. This is one of the best ways to begin.

Finishing threads This is best done by weaving the thread through the back of the existing stitching as invisibly as possible. (Some embroiderers recommend that you work a small back stitch at the end). Trim the end neatly.

Getting the Right Tension

Tension is all-important for pulled thread work. The pulled thread stitches (pages 22–50) need to be drawn up tight so that they force the fabric into shape. Just how tightly you work these stitches depends on how you want the final stitch to look. The tighter you pull, the lacier the effect.

If in doubt, sample the stitch on a scrap of your chosen fabric first to see what you like best. Always work a particular stitch in the same tension throughout the piece or the result will look messy.

Most of the complementary stitches on pages 55–63 should be worked so that they lie smoothly on the fabric without pulling it.

When to start pulling If you are beginning with the darning method (see above) and you are not changing the angle of the thread too much you can usually start pulling on the first stitch. If you are beginning in a new area using the waste knot method you have two choices. Usually you can start with an unpulled stitch and then start pulling on the second stitch. In many cases this looks more natural than trying to pull up the first stitch. Alternatively you can work a small stitch, known as a tacking

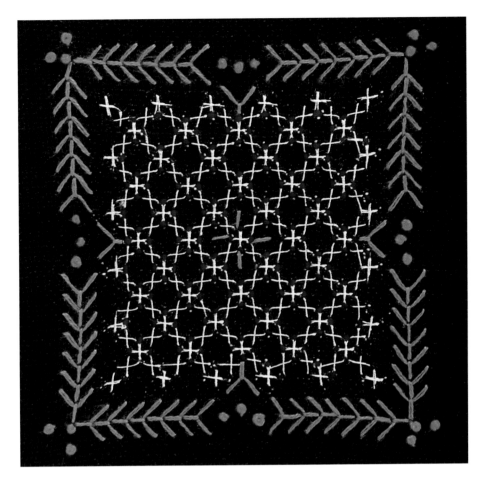

■ *In Festive Lace (page 29) Coats Ophir metallic thread adds shimmer for a luxurious touch. French knots for the berries provide additional form and texture. However, these could easily be replaced with beads, if preferred.*

stitch, over a thread of fabric beside the starting point. This way you can start pulling from the very first stitch but this is only practical if the thread matches the fabric so the stitch is inconspicuous. What looks best often depends on the type of stitch being worked and this is really a question of trial and error.

Turning When you start a new row or turn a corner the final stitch of the last row and the first stitch of the new row may pull each other out of shape. To avoid this you can either take a tacking stitch over a single thread of fabric or work a back stitch

through the back of an adjacent stitch before you begin the new row, or you can leave these two stitches unpulled.

Partial Stitches

The diagrams in this book indicate how to work each stitch in a straightforward situation such as in a sampler. However, in many designs you will find that you need to fill a complex shape. In this case you may need to work some partial stitches (compensating stitches) around the edges of the motif. If you have designed your own piece, work the full stitches first and then work the partial stitches as best as you can to give the look of the stitch continuing beyond the design area.

In this book all the designs are shown at full size, or sometimes larger, alongside their charts, making it easier for you to see exactly what has been done.

Adding Beads

Beads add shimmer, texture and an extra dimension to your embroidery. You can add these in place of any of the complementary stitches (see pages 55–63), such as French knots or even a whole line of chain stitch. They are easy to attach with ordinary sewing thread simply by threading one on in the marked position and working a back stitch over one or two threads of the fabric. If your beads have fine holes it may be necessary to use a beading needle or switch to a finer thread. However, do make sure that the thread is strong enough to secure the beads properly. (Usually polyester mix thread is stronger than pure cotton thread.)

Choose beads that match the size of the stitch you are replacing in order to maintain the balance of the design. Seed beads are ideal for 28-count evenweave fabric.

Finishing Your Embroidery

Working the final stitch in an embroidery is very satisfying but it doesn't mean that you have finished. You still have to turn your stitching into an item that can be displayed. This may mean mounting and framing it, hemming the edges or stitching the embroidered fabric to other pieces of fabric and making it up into something else.

Mounting and Framing

Framing an embroidery yourself usually saves money and is more satisfying than handing it over to someone else to do, but if you have put a lot of work into the embroidery and aren't particularly handy then you may wish to prepare it for framing and then get a professional to finish the job.

The first step is to decide on the frame and mount (mat) sizes. Start with the size of the finished embroidery. The aperture of the mount should be 1–2.5cm (½–1in) bigger all round than a small embroidery design and up to 5cm (2in) bigger all round than a large design. The mount is usually 5–10cm (2–4in) larger all round than this, though sometimes a larger mount can look excellent. If you are framing the design yourself you'll need to adapt the finished size you have calculated to the nearest size of ready-made frame. You may be lucky enough to find a mount at the frame suppliers that is perfect for your design and frame. If not many framers will cut a mount for you to your specifications.

If desired, you can make the mount more interesting by covering it with fabric or one of the many attractive crafters' papers available today. If you wish to use paper, make sure it is acid-free, like the ones that are designed for use in photograph albums. Covering a standard mount is quite easy but you need to take some care when dealing with the corners of the aperture. Cut the paper or fabric 2cm (¾in) larger all round, apply a little glue to the front of the mount and press the paper on. (Spray Mount or glue stick are ideal.) Refer to Covering an Oval Mount, opposite, to fold the outside edges to the back and glue in place. Snip to the corners of the aperture from the centre and trim and then glue these edges in place too. For a mount with an oval aperture simply follow the steps shown right.

The next stage is to lace your embroidery to a piece of thick card or mount board that fits your chosen frame. To cushion and protect the embroidery it is a good idea to glue lightweight polyester wadding (fleece) to the card or board using white craft glue (PVA). Once this is dry, follow the steps above right to lace your work to the board.

■ *This nautical design (see page 49) has been enhanced with a coordinating fabric-covered mount, giving it greater impact.*

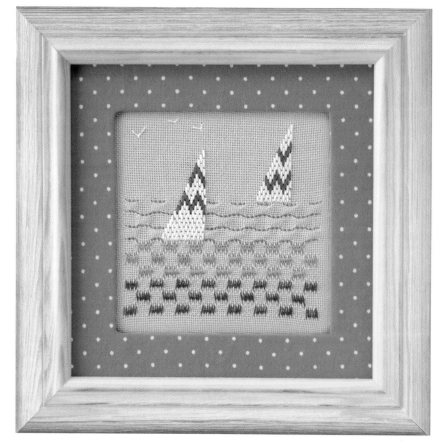

Lacing Your Work

LACING YOUR WORK to board or card is an essential first stage in framing your embroidery. This keeps the embroidery smooth and neat in the frame for professional results. Using a padded board helps to cushion and protect the stitching.

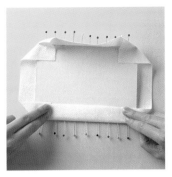

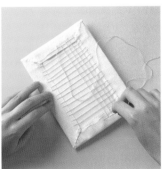

Fig 1. Cut the fabric so it extends 2.5–5cm (1–2in) beyond the card or board edges and mark the finished size with tacking (basting). Lay it face down on a clean, dry surface and place the card padded-side down on top, using the tacking (basting) stitches as a guide to placement. Pin the fabric to one long edge of the card with the pins about 1cm (3/8in) apart. Pulling the fabric so it lies smooth, pin the opposite edge. Fold in the corners of the fabric diagonally to mitre them, as shown, then pin the remaining edges.

Fig 2. Turn the embroidery over and check that the fabric is taut and correctly positioned. Turn it back over. Thread a large needle with enough strong thread to lace the long edges of the fabric together. Lace these edges by taking a stitch about 1cm (3/8in) on one side and then a stitch of the same length on the other side. Every few stitches check that the lacing is tight. When you reach the end, knot off and start a new thread to lace the remaining sides together. Oversew each of the mitred corners to finish and then mount your work in the frame.

Covering an Oval Mount

COVERING AN OVAL MOUNT is easier than you may think and it gives your work an additional handcrafted look. In a way it is easier to cover an oval mount than a rectangular one because you do not have to deal with the corners of the aperture, which can be quite difficult to cover neatly.

Fig 1. Cut the paper or fabric 2cm (3/4in) larger all round than the mount (mat) and lay it face down. Apply stick glue or spray, such as Spray Mount, to the mount and lay it glue-side down centrally on the paper/fabric. Turn the mount over and smooth out any air bubbles, then turn it back over. Turn the corners of the paper/fabric over the mount diagonally, as shown, and secure them with tape or glue. Now turn over the straight edges, secure with glue and tape the mitred corners for added security.

Fig 2. Cut the centre of the paper/fabric away, leaving a 2cm (3/4in) margin around the mount aperture. Snip into the paper/fabric edges at 12mm (1/2in) intervals, cutting close to but not right up to the mount. Run glue stick around the inner edge of the mount and fold back the tabs of fabric or paper, pressing each one firmly on to the mount. Apply masking tape as well for added security.

Embroidery Ideas

All the designs in this book would make lovely framed pictures, notably the sampler on page 52, and this is often the starting point for any embroidery lover. But this is by no means the whole story. Pulled thread embroidery can be worked on any evenweave fabric in any colour, and this can then be made up into all manner of useful items for the home. Popular projects include tea cosies, tray cloths, napkins and place mats (see page 18) as well as curtain tiebacks, needle cases and all types of bags. You'll find instructions for making a useful shopping bag on page 21.

Your embroidered piece can also be stitched to other fabrics, opening up further possibilities. One simple idea is to make it into a pocket that can be stitched on to a ready-made item of clothing such as a shirt, dress or dungarees. Alternatively, you can make your own item from scratch, such as the pretty apron shown opposite and on page 19.

If you have already stitched your embroidery and wish to display it in an interesting way, a really good idea is to turn it into the centrepiece of a patchwork cushion. Combine it with fabrics that tie in with the colours of the embroidery but preferably have fairly subtle patterns that won't take attention away from your embroidery. You'll find instructions for making such a cushion on page 20. Alternatively, you could back your embroidery with a piece of similar fabric and turn it into a pincushion or scented sachet.

All of the projects on the following pages are simple to make and, apart from the apron, do not require much sewing experience, so they are suitable for beginners or the more experienced. Feel free to use any of the designs in this book in place of the ones chosen for each project. For example, the pineapple design from page 47 would work well on the place mat and the dragonfly (page 43) would look lovely on the bag or apron.

■ *A place mat is an ideal project for pulled thread work, enabling you to display your embroidery for all to see, and you can make a set utilizing several of the designs from this book. Another nice idea is to make a pocket for an apron, such as the grapes pocket shown here. Instructions for both these designs and more are given on the following pages.*

Place Mat

Materials

- 50 x 40cm (20 x 16in) piece of Anchor 28-count Jobelan in white
- 1 x 5g ball of Anchor Pearl Cotton No.12 in white
- 1 skein of Anchor Stranded Cotton in green (241)
- 1 skein each of Anchor Marlitt in medium red (893) and deep red (894)
- Needles, pins and scissors

Matching Napkin

Cut a 40cm (16in) square of 28-count Anchor Jobelan for each napkin and work your design. Remove the cross threads from each edge for 2.5cm (1in) to make a generous fringe.

This place mat measures 36 x 26cm (14 x 10in). Make a set using the same design or substitute other designs from this book for variety. The pineapple from page 47 would work particularly well as would the champagne glasses from page 35. This idea could also be adapted to make a tray cloth and matching napkins.

Following the chart on page 27, work the strawberry motif approximately 10cm (4in) from the bottom and right-hand edges of your fabric using the colours listed in the key. Work the border as shown on the chart, extending it to a rectangle 30 x 20cm (12 x 8in) and working the heart, leaf and eyelet motifs in the corners only.

Count 14 threads out from each edge of the border and carefully snip through the next four fabric threads on each side at the centre. Use the point of a needle to unweave the first cut thread and discard. Unweave the second cut thread to a point 4cm (1½in) beyond the embroidery. Thread it on to a needle and weave it

Alternative Hem

If you find the idea of withdrawing threads too daunting, you can make an alternative hem by turning the excess fabric to the right side, mitring the corners neatly, and then covering the raw edges with coordinating ribbon, also mitred. Machine stitch the ribbon in place with matching thread along both long edges.

into the channel left by the removal of the first thread between this point and the fabric edge. Make sure it lies flat and do not pull too hard or you will distort the edge of your band. Repeat with the third and fourth cut threads and the remaining sides.

Trim the outer edges of the embroidery to leave a 2cm (¾in) border beyond the channel left by the withdrawn threads. Fold under the edge twice by 1cm (³/₈in), mitring the corners and pin or tack (baste) in place. Using white Anchor Pearl Cotton No. 12, work ladder hemstitch along the withdrawn thread channel (see page 59), catching the folded fabric edge.

Remove any pins or tacking stitches remaining and press the finished place mat carefully from the wrong side.

Apron

Materials

- 40 x 30cm (16 x 12in) piece of Anchor 28-count Jobelan in Prairie green or a colour to match your fabric
- 1 skein each of Anchor Stranded Cotton in pale violet (870), medium violet (872), dark sea green (877), very dark sea green (879), pale mauve (1018) and dark mauve (1019)
- 1m (1yd) coordinating printed cotton fabric
- 1m (1yd) bias binding 1.5cm (½in) wide
- 2m (2yd) cotton tape 2.5cm (1in) wide cut into three equal lengths
- Sewing cotton
- Needles, pins and scissors

Apron Pattern

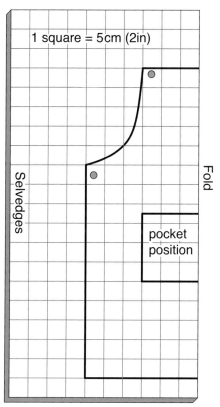

1 square = 5cm (2in)

Selvedges

Fold

pocket position

Measuring approximately 77 x 54cm (30 x 21in) excluding the straps, this apron should keep you covered in the kitchen, although you may be tempted to keep it for best.

Following the chart on page 23, work three bunches of grapes across the centre of the fabric. Offset the centre bunch by ten fabric threads downwards and omit some tendrils to allow for close spacing of the motifs. Use 870 and 872 for the centre bunch and 1018 and 1019 for the outer bunches. Use 877 and 879 for all leaves and tendrils.

Measure 5cm (2in) from the top of the embroidery. Carefully snip through the next four horizontal fabric threads and remove them with a needle. Trim the top of the fabric, leaving a border of 2cm (¾in) above the withdrawn threads. Fold the raw edge under twice by 1cm (³⁄₈in) and pin. Trim the embroidery to 34 x 22cm (13½ x 8½in). Using one strand of 877, work ladder hemstitch along the withdrawn thread area, catching the folded hem. Turn under 1.5cm (⁵⁄₈in) twice around the remaining raw edges and press

carefully from the wrong side. Tack (baste) or pin in place.

Enlarge the apron pattern and cut from folded cotton fabric. Neaten the curved edges with bias binding. Turn a 1cm (³⁄₈in) double hem along the remaining edges and pin or tack (baste). Pin the end of one piece of tape to the lower dot at each side of the apron and the third piece at the top, one end at each top dot. Stitch the hems and tape in place.

Position the embroidered pocket on the apron and pin. Try on the apron to check the fit and adjust if necessary. Stitch the pocket to the apron around the sides and lower edge. Work a second line of machine stitching 1cm (³⁄₈in) from the edge for strength.

Patchwork Cushion

Materials

- 20cm (8in) square of Anchor 28-count Jobelan in pale green or the colour of your choice

- 1 skein each of Anchor Stranded Cotton in cerise (62), violet (98), pewter (236), medium sea green (876), pale sea green (1042) and blue/pink multicolor (1325)

- Two fat quarters of coordinating cotton fabrics (available from quilting stores)

- Matching thread

- Needles, pins and scissors

This cushion fits a 38cm (15in) cushion pad and is made from a simple patchwork of nine pieces. You can easily adapt it to fit a cushion of any size (see the tip below), coordinating the fabrics and stitching to suit your décor. Use the hydrangea design from page 31 or any other design in this book.

Work the hydrangea design from page 31 in the centre of the Jobelan. Trim the embroidery with the design still centred to 12.5cm (5in) square. Neaten the edges with machine zigzag to prevent fraying.

Cut four 12.5cm (5in) squares from each of your printed cottons and from one of the fabrics cut two 25 x 36cm (10 x 14in) rectangles for the cushion back.

Join the fabric squares to form the patchwork using the photograph as a guide and taking scant 1cm (3/8in) seam allowances. Press the seams open. Turn under and stitch a 1cm (3/8in) hem along one long edge of each rectangle of fabric. Press the hems. Lay out the patchwork cushion front and lay the two rectangles on top, right sides down, with their hemmed edges overlapping at the centre and the raw edges matching. If necessary, trim the edges of the back pieces to match the front piece. Now tack the layers together around the edges and then stitch all round, taking a 1cm (3/8in) seam allowance.

Trim the seam allowances diagonally at the corners and turn the cushion cover out through the gap in the back. Press lightly, if necessary. Insert the cushion pad.

Changing the Size

To make this cushion cover to fit an existing pad first divide the length and width of the pad by three. For a 30cm (12in) square pad this gives 10cm (4in). Add 1cm (¼in) for each seam allowance and cut each of your nine squares to your new measurement (12cm/4¾in). Make up the cushion front then cut out the back pieces the same width as the front and two thirds of the height.

Shopping Bag

Shopping will be a lot more fun with this pretty bag, which has been decorated with the design on page 47. The body of the bag is made from calico, which is inexpensive, yet strong, but if you prefer you can use canvas or any other strong cotton fabric.

design on page 47

Materials

- 40cm (16in) square of Anchor 28-count Jobelan in ivory
- One skein each of Anchor Stranded Cotton in pale yellow (300) and pistachio (241)
- One skein each of Anchor Marlitt in yellow (848) and pale yellow (1012)
- 50cm (½yd) unbleached calico fabric 150cm (60in) wide
- Sewing cotton
- Needles, pins and scissors

Following the chart on page 47, work the pineapple motif in the centre of the Jobelan. Press the finished embroidery carefully from the wrong side. With the design still centred, trim the fabric to 30cm (12in) square. Turn under a 2cm (¾in) hem along each side edge of the Jobelan; tack (baste) in place. Turn a 2cm (¾in) hem along the top edge and this time stitch it in place. Press gently.

From calico cut two 40 x 50cm (16 x 20in) pieces for the bag front and back. Cut two 10 x 50cm (4 x 20in) strips for the handles. Fold the handles in half lengthways and stitch the long edge taking a 1cm (³⁄₈in) seam allowance. Turn the strips out and press the seam to the centre of one side.

Take one of the large pieces of calico and turn under a 2cm

(¾in) hem on one short edge; press. This edge will be at the top of the bag. Take a handle and position one end 10cm (4in) from one raw side edge so that the right side of the handle (without the seam) faces the wrong side of the bag. Repeat with the other end of the handle, positioning it 10cm (4in) from the other side edge. Pin in place. Stitch the top hem of the bag, catching the handles. Sew a second line of stitching close to the top edge of the bag for strength. Neaten the remaining raw edges of the bag piece with machine zigzag.

Centre the embroidery on the lower edge of the bag piece with raw edges matching. Pin in place. Stitch along both side edges of the embroidery, leaving the top edge open to form a pocket.

Fold a 2cm (¾in) hem on the remaining bag piece and attach the the handle to the top edge in the same way as before. Neaten the remaining raw edges. Fold the back of the bag over so that the raw edges of the two bag pieces match and right sides are facing. Stitch together around the sides and lower edge, taking a 1.5cm (½in) seam allowance. Snip the seam allowances at the corners for ease and then turn the completed bag right sides out and press lightly.

Handle Options

The handles on this bag are easy to make and won't cost a penny, but there are many other options for the more adventurous. For example, you could plait three 1m (39in) lengths of coloured cord together for each handle or do the same with tubes of fabric (rouleaux) padded with lengths of wool or cord. You can even buy ready-made handles from craft suppliers in plastic or leather for a touch of luxury.

Algerian Filling Stitch

ALGERIAN FILLING STITCH is simply satin stitch worked in stepped blocks. Each block is made up of three stitches worked over four fabric threads. Work in horizontal rows, stitching alternate blocks as explained here and pulling the stitches firmly. This stitch is used to fill the centre of the Art Deco Rose, page 41.

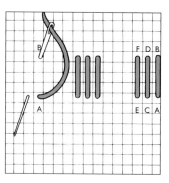

Fig 1. Bring the needle out at A and insert it at B, four fabric threads above it. Repeat to bring the needle out at C and go in at D, out at E and back in at F. Begin the next group four threads to the left and continue in the same way to the end of the line.

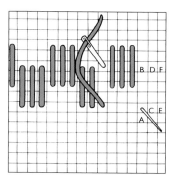

Fig 2. Work the next row from left to right, stepping the blocks down two threads of fabric and placing them between the blocks of the previous row. Repeat these two rows to fill the area.

Back Stitch, Ringed

RINGED BACK STITCH is simply back stitch worked in an octagonal shape – a ring. It is worked from right to left as a series of half rings, which are completed on the return journey. The connecting stitches between the rings are worked into the same holes. All stitches must be pulled firmly. This stitch is used for the grapes in the design shown opposite.

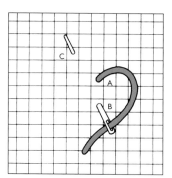

Fig 1. Bring the needle out at A, insert it at B, two threads down, and bring it out at C.

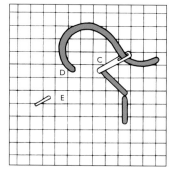

Fig 2. Insert the needle at A and bring it out at D, in at C and out at E.

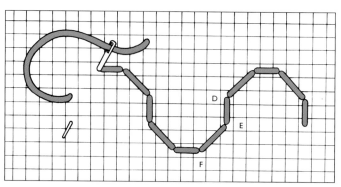

Fig 3. Continue on round to complete a half-ring then work a half ring pointing downwards, then another one facing up and so on. Turn the fabric round and repeat in mirror image to complete the rings.

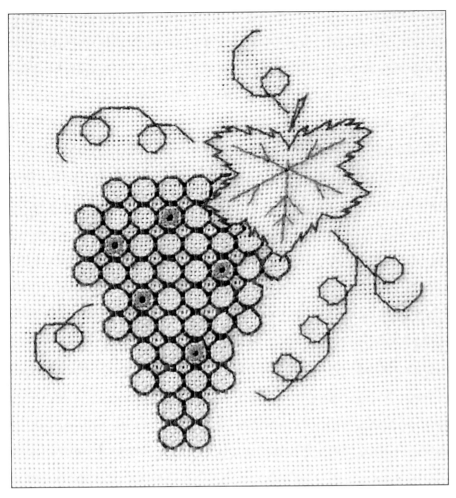

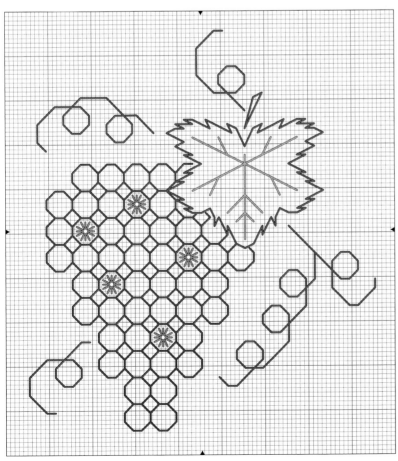
Grapes

Work this lovely design on napkins or a tablecloth or on any item to be displayed in a dining room or conservatory. It was stitched on 28-count white Jobelan, but you can use any similar alternative fabric such as Anchor Evenweave fabric. Use two strands of thread unless otherwise stated. Work the grapes in ringed back stitch (opposite) using 872, with eyelets (page 32) in 870 for variation and texture. Outline the leaves in Holbein stitch (page 60) using one strand of 877 and work the veins in 876. Work the tendrils and leaf stalk in the same stitch using a single strand of 877.

NOTE:
On this chart the gridlines represent individual fabric threads.

KEY

ANCHOR STRANDED
COTTON (FLOSS)

	870		876
	872		877

FINISHED SIZE
8 x 8cm (3¼ x 3¼in)

Chequer Filling Stitch

CHEQUER FILLING STITCH creates a pretty, lacy design. It is worked diagonally first one way and then the other, with the stitches pulled firmly. It can be worked as single rows or to cover large areas and is used in the Wedding Sampler on page 52 within the heart motif at the top of the design.

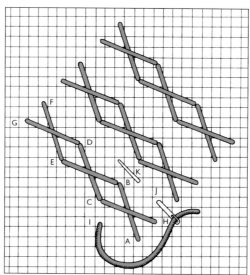

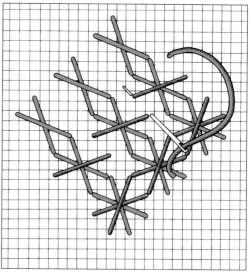

Fig 1. Bring the needle out at A and insert it at B (six threads up and two threads to the left). Bring the needle back out at C and go in at D. Continue making half cross stitches to the end of the line, then work back, completing the oblong crosses. Work further rows, until the whole area is covered. Now bring the needle out at I, and insert it at J, bringing it back out at K.

Fig 2. Repeat to work a line of half crosses over the oblong crosses, then complete these new crosses on the return journey. This diagram shows the progression of the stitch for easy reference.

Chessboard Filling

CHESSBOARD FILLING is worked over blocks of nine threads, each block being worked with three bands of satin stitch. The stitches are pulled tight to create three bars, and because the blocks are worked in alternate directions this gives the look of woven fabric, as on the basket of the design opposite.

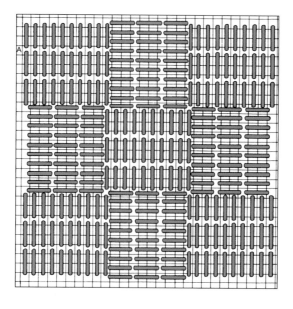

Bring the needle out at A. Work a row of ten vertical satin stitches, each one over three fabric threads. Pull each stitch tightly to gather in the fabric threads. Work two more rows directly beneath the first so that the stitches of each row share the holes of the satin stitches above. Work the next block of three satin stitch rows vertically, the next horizontally, and so on, to complete the effect.

Flower Basket

Chessboard filling (opposite), worked in two strands of light brown Anchor Stranded Cotton (392) gives this basket real texture so that you might almost pick it up. It is worked in a darker shade of the background fabric (tan Jobelan) in the traditional way and this allows the bright flowers to stand out. Use two strands of the same colour for the handle, working in long-armed cross stitch (page 61). Still using two strands throughout, work the large flowers as Milanese Pinwheels (page 61) in 301 and 302 and work the smaller flowers in octagonal Rhodes stitch (page 62) using 324. Complete the design with the leaves, worked in leaf stitch (page 60) using 267.

NOTE:

On this chart the gridlines represent individual fabric threads.

KEY

ANCHOR STRANDED
COTTON (FLOSS)

 267   324

 301   392

 302

FINISHED SIZE

8 x 9cm (3¼ x 3½in)

Cobbler Filling

COBBLER FILLING is an incredibly easy stitch to work being composed of straight stitches that are worked in pairs. Provided that you count the threads correctly, there are no pitfalls with this stitch and the result is a beautiful textured effect as featured on the lower wings of the dragonfly on page 43.

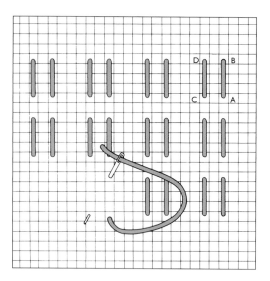

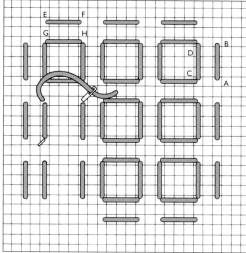

Fig 1. Work all the vertical stitches in rows. Each stitch should be worked over four threads, leaving alternately two and then four threads between each. Bring the needle out at A, insert it at B, bring it out at C and insert it at D. Continue working in this way. Leave a gap of two threads between rows.

Fig 2. Work the horizontal stitches in the spaces between the vertical stitches to form squares, as shown. Bring the needle out at E, insert it at F, bring it out at G and insert it at H. Continue working in this way until the full area is completed.

Coil Filling

COIL FILLING pulls the fabric threads into a pattern of stars if worked in matching thread or crosses if worked in contrast thread. It is worked by simply stitching clusters of three vertical satin stitches into the same holes. Pull each stitch firmly to ensure the desired result, as shown on the strawberry of the design opposite.

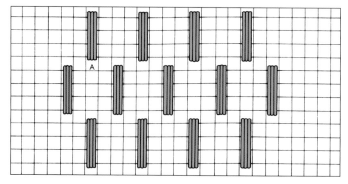

Beginning at A, work three satin stitches over the required number of horizontal fabric threads, in this case four. Leave a gap of the same number of vertical fabric threads. Repeat to the end. Take a small stitch into the back of the last cluster of each row to secure it. Work the next row staggered midway between the stitches of the previous row, as shown.

Stitching Notes

Strawberry

Work this design over two strands of white Anchor Jobelan. Work the outline of the large strawberry with whipped back stitch (page 55) in red Marlitt (894) and its leaves in leaf stitch (page 60) using green Anchor Stranded Cotton (241). Work coil filling inside the strawberry in 894 and 893. Outline the border in running stitch, then work the hearts with satin stitch (page 63) using 894. Work the leaves in leaf stitch variation (page 60) using 241 and work the diamond eyelets (page 32) in the border in white Anchor Pearl Cotton No. 12.

NOTE:
On this chart the gridlines represent individual fabric threads.

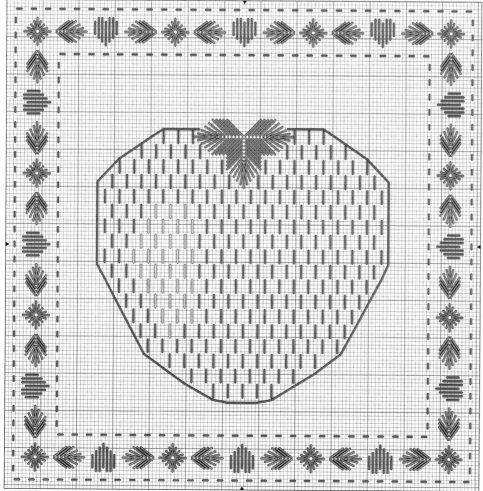

KEY

ANCHOR PEARL
COTTON NO. 12

White

KEY

ANCHOR STRANDED
COTTON (FLOSS)

241

ANCHOR MARLITT

893   894

FINISHED SIZE
9.5 x 9cm (3¾ x 3½in)

Pulled Thread Stitches 27

Diagonal Raised Band Filling

DIAGONAL RAISED BAND FILLING creates a very open effect, similar to the look of filet crochet. It is worked in a series of diagonal crosses, each stitch being firmly pulled to achieve an open effect. You can see this stitch in the Art Deco Rose, page 41, where it is used for the leaves.

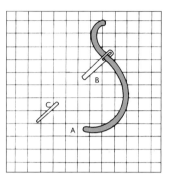

Fig 1. Bring the needle out at A, insert it at B (four threads up) and bring it out at C, two threads to the left and two threads up from A.

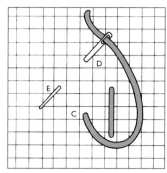

Fig 2. Insert the needle at D (four threads up) and bring it out at E. Continue working in this way to cover the whole area.

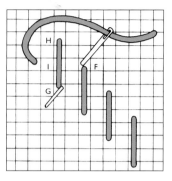

Fig 3. After completing the last stitch at H, bring the needle through at I, insert the needle at F and bring it out at G in readiness for the next stitch. Complete all the crosses, pulling each stitch tight as you go. Work the next diagonal row so it touches the first.

Diagonal Raised Band Filling: Open Trellis

THE OPEN TRELLIS variation is basically diagonal raised band filling worked over six threads of fabric. Gaps are left between the rows to leave unstitched squares and create a totally new look. Another variation is shown on page 30, showing you what you can achieve simply by altering the size and position of a basic stitch. This stitch features in the centre of the Festive Lace design opposite.

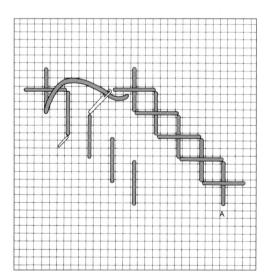

Fig 1. Beginning at A, work rows of diagonal raised band filling as above but work over six threads and space the rows six threads apart, as shown.

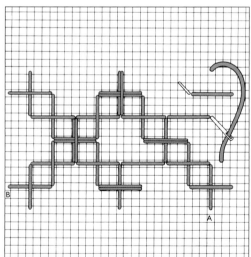

Fig 2. To create the trellis pattern, begin at B and work rows of diagonal raised bands in the opposite direction, crossing the previous rows of stitches at regular intervals. This time work the horizontal stitches first. Where the rows intersect, work on top of the previous row to form double stitches.

Stitching Notes

Festive Lace

This festive design would make a wonderful Christmas tree ornament or card or it could be worked on a Christmas stocking or other seasonal item. It was worked on black Anchor Jobelan for a dramatic effect, which makes the colours stand out like jewels. Use one strand of gold Coats Ophir to work the centre of the design in diagonal raised band open trellis filling (opposite). Then use two strands of Anchor Stranded Cotton (floss) to work the leafy border in fly stitch (page 58) in 228 and to work the berries in French knots (page 59) in 46. Add the straight stitches in the centre in 228. If desired, back the piece in a coloured fabric to show through the holes.

NOTE:
On this chart the gridlines represent individual fabric threads.

KEY

ANCHOR STRANDED
COTTON (FLOSS)

 228   46

COATS OPHIR

300

FINISHED SIZE
8 x 7.5cm (3¼ x 3in)

Diagonal Raised Band Filling Variation

THIS DIAGONAL RAISED BAND FILLING VARIATION has each cross worked over six fabric threads with the rows spaced four threads apart. It creates distinct diagonal bands of holes in the fabric or, when worked in a contrasting thread distinct diagonal crosses. You can see this stitch in the Frosted Fields design on page 33 where it is used for the rear field.

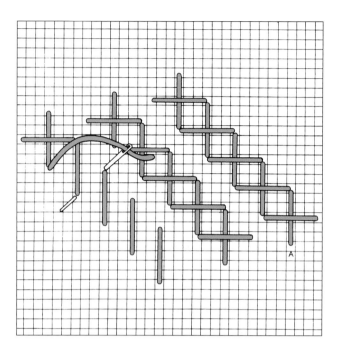

Bring the needle out at A. Work a series of vertical straight stitches stepped in the same way as diagonal raised band filling (page 28) but with the stitches worked over six fabric threads. Leave four threads between diagonal rows. Now work the horizontal stitches, pulling up each stitch to a tight, even tension.

Diagonal Satin Filling

DIAGONAL SATIN FILLING pulls the fabric to create a pattern of large and small holes with dense fillings between them. Each block of four resembles a four-petalled flower but blocks can be worked in any formation – singly, in rows or groups. In the Blue Hydrangea design opposite the filling is massed to give texture to the flower head.

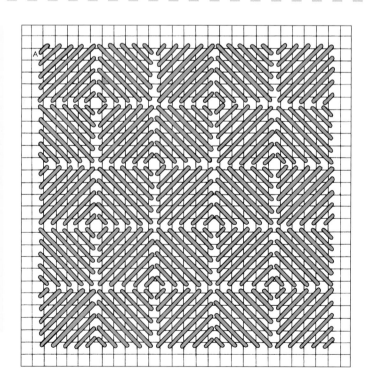

Bring the needle out at A and work a block of diagonal satin stitch (page 63) over an area of 5 x 5 fabric threads, as shown. Work the second block with the stitches slanting in the opposite direction. Continue in this way, alternating the direction of stitches for each block. Stitches must be firmly pulled to achieve the effect.

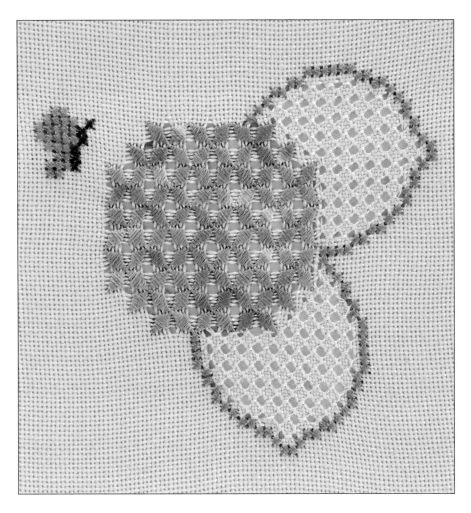

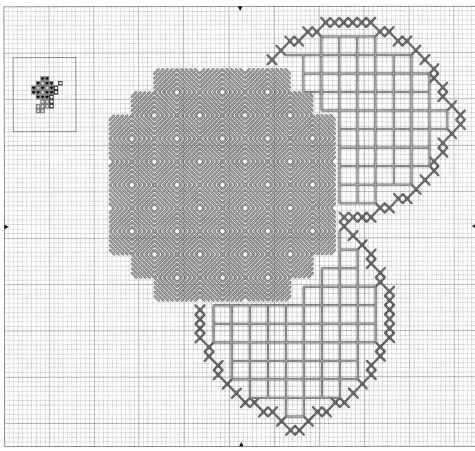

Blue Hydrangea

Work this design over two strands of pale green Anchor Jobelan. Use pink/purple Anchor Multicolor Stranded Cotton (1325) to stitch the flower in diagonal satin filling, Work the leaf outlines with cross stitch using two strands of 877. Fill them with punch stitch (page 46) using 1042 to match the fabric. Finally work the butterfly in cross stitch using 403 for the body, with 62 and 97 for the upper and lower wings.

NOTE:
On this chart the gridlines represent individual fabric threads except for the butterfly. Here each block represents one cross stitch worked over two intersecting fabric threads.

KEY

ANCHOR STRANDED
COTTON (FLOSS)

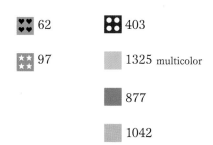

62   403

97   1325 multicolor

877

1042

FINISHED SIZE
7.5 x 8cm (3 x 3¼in)

Diamond Eyelet

DIAMOND EYELET is formed by working a series of satin stitches around a central hole in a diamond shape. A simple variation is eyelet hole, which is worked in a square. The tighter you pull the stitching, the larger the hole becomes, so decide what effect you want before you begin. Diamond eyelets feature in Frosted Fields opposite, while eyelets are used in the border of the Strawberry design on page 27.

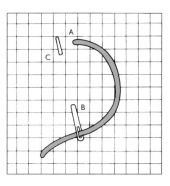

Fig 1. Bring the needle out at A, insert it at B where the centre of the eyelet will be and bring it out again at C.

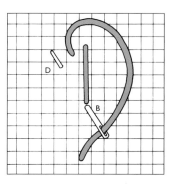

Fig 2. Insert the needle at B again and bring it out at D, as shown.

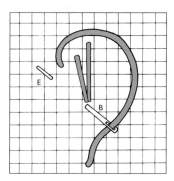

Fig 3. Insert the needle at B and bring it out at E. Continue working in this sequence around the central hole, B, to complete the diamond eyelet.

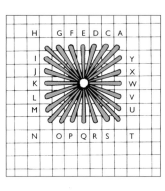

Fig 4. To work an eyelet hole start in the upper right-hand corner of the eyelet and work round it in a square formation, as shown.

Diamond Filling

DIAMOND FILLING is produced by working double back stitch (see page 34) in stepped lines to make zigzag rows. Two zigzag rows are worked to form a diamond pattern, which covers a large area quite quickly. It is ideal for borders or samplers, as shown on page 52.

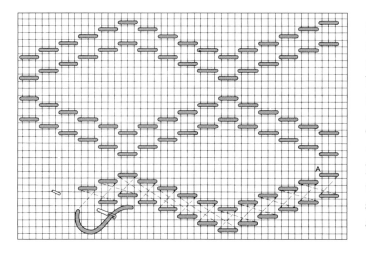

Begin at A, working over the same number of fabric threads throughout. The broken lines in the diagram indicate the thread lying on the back of the fabric. The proportions of the 'diamonds' can be varied by lengthening or shortening the zigzag lines. Stitches should be pulled firmly for an open effect.

Stitching Notes

Frosted Fields

Use two strands of thread unless otherwise stated. Work on pewter Anchor Jobelan. Work the foreground field in Greek cross square filling (page 42) using 398 with crosses of 301 in the gaps. For the distant field use diagonal raised band variation (page 30) in 399. Use satin stitch (page 63) to work the bushes in 877 and work the buildings in 399. Use fern stitch (page 57) for the trees behind the rear field. Work the frosty diamond eyelets (page 32) in white and silver.

NOTE:
On this chart the gridlines represent individual fabric threads.

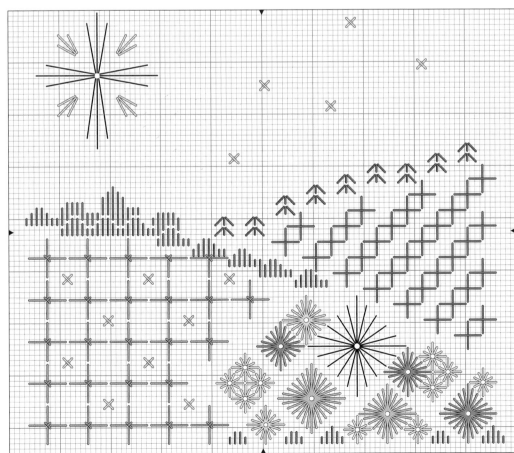

KEY

ANCHOR STRANDED
COTTON (FLOSS)

▢	1	▨	399
▨	398	▨	877

COATS REFLECTA

▢ 301

ANCHOR PEARL COTTON

■ 1 (No. 5 metallic)   ▢ 1 (No. 12)

ANCHOR MARLITT

▨ 800

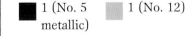

FINISHED SIZE
8 x 8cm (3¼ x 3¼in)

Double Back Stitch: Finnish Filling

DOUBLE BACK STITCH is a useful stitch because it can be viewed from both sides. On the front it creates parallel lines of back stitch while on the back it resembles a close herringbone. In figure 5 it is arranged to form Finnish filling, which is used in Champagne Celebration, opposite, to capture the bubbly liquid in the glasses.

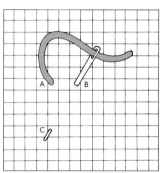

Fig 1. Bring the needle out at A and insert it at B, two threads to the right. Bring it out again at C, directly below A and four threads down.

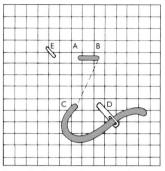

Fig 2. Insert the needle at D, in line with both B and C and bring it out at E.

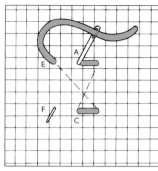

Fig 3. Insert the needle at A and bring it out at F.

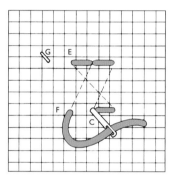

Fig 4. Insert the needle at C and bring it out at G. Continue repeating steps 3 and 4 to complete the line.

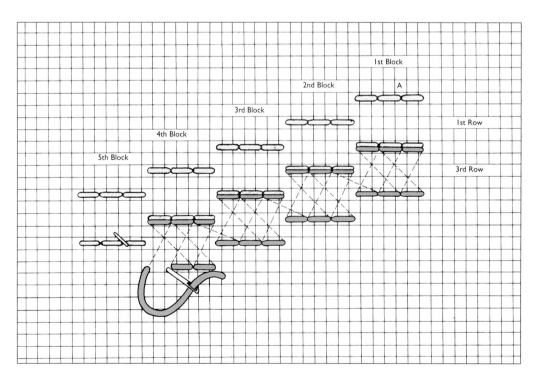

Fig 5. To work Finnish filling work a stepped line of double back stitches. Work a second row directly below the first and repeat until the area is covered. This gives the fabric a mesh-like appearance.

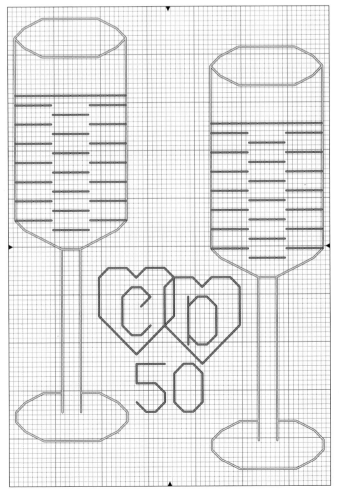

Champagne Celebration

Finnish filling worked in gold Coats Reflecta (300) creates sparkling champagne bubbles in this design, which celebrates a golden wedding anniversary. It was stitched on cream 28-count Anchor Jobelan for an elegant look. For a silver wedding anniversary you could work in silver thread on blue fabric. Work the outline of the glasses first in whipped back stitch (page 55) using a single strand of 387 for the back stitch and gold Coats Reflecta (300) for the whipping. Work the hearts, initials and number in back stitch, referring to the alphabet chart on page 54. Finally work the filling in Coats Reflecta (300).

NOTE:
On this chart the gridlines represent individual fabric threads.

KEY

ANCHOR PEARL
COTTON NO. 8

■ 387

COATS REFLECTA

■ 300

FINISHED SIZE
9 x 6cm (3½ x 2½in)

Double Faggot Filling

DOUBLE FAGGOT FILLING re-creates the look of fillet lace when worked in a matching thread but can also be worked in a colour, if desired. Its name comes from the word faggot, meaning bundle of fire wood because the small straight stitches are bundled or grouped to make the design. It is used for the main filling in the Cherry Blossom design, opposite.

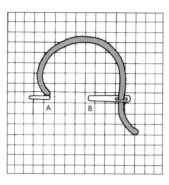

Fig 1. Bring the needle out at A, insert it at B, four threads to the right, and bring it back out at A.

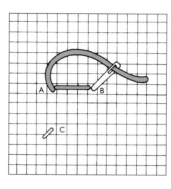

Fig 2. Take the needle back in at B and bring it out at C, four threads below A.

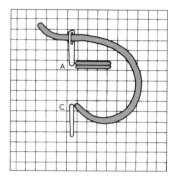

Fig 3. Insert the needle at A and bring it out at C.

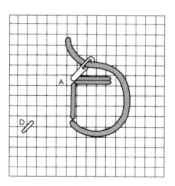

Fig 4. Re-insert the needle at A and bring it through at D.

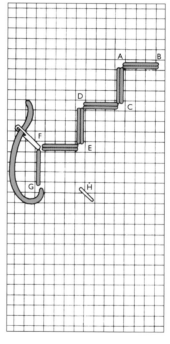

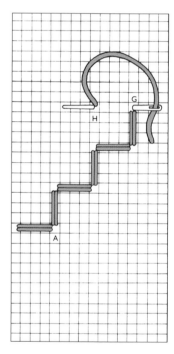

Fig 5. Continue in this way following the alphabetical sequence to the end of the diagonal row. Bring the needle out at H and turn the work upside down.

Fig 6. Insert the needle at G and bring it back out at H. Continue as before to create a diagonal row of squares. Work subsequent rows in the same way.

■ *Keep a Count*
When working on a design such as Cherry Blossom (opposite) where it is vital to position the corner motifs correctly, make sure that you count over the shortest possible distance of unstitched fabric to avoid losing count.

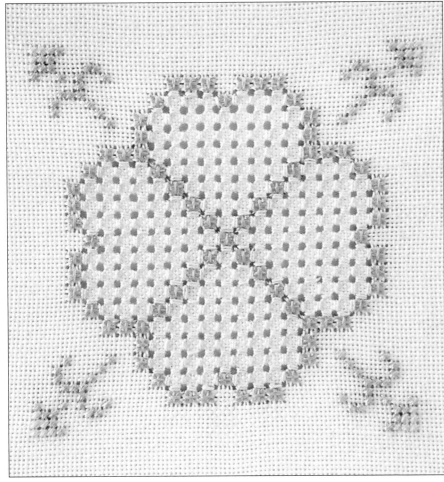

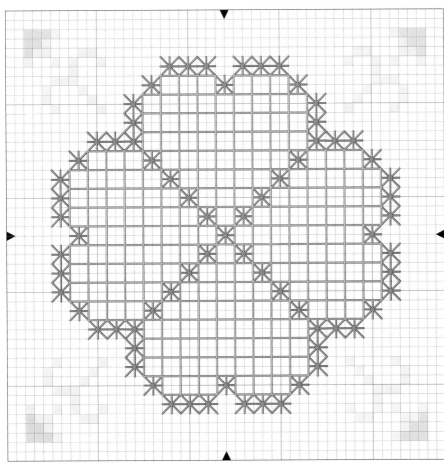

Cherry Blossom

This pretty design was inspired by spring cherry blossom and is worked on white Anchor Jobelan in shades of pink. It shows how several different thread types can be utilized to add subtle variety to your stitching. Start with the outline of the large flower, using two strands of pink Anchor Marlitt (813) to work double cross stitch (page 57). Fill the flower with double faggot filling (opposite), worked in one strand of Anchor Pearl Cotton in 48. Work the smaller motifs in the corners in cross stitch (page 56), using two strands of 206 for the leaves and stems and 48 for the flower buds.

NOTE:
On this chart each square represents a block of 2 x 2 fabric threads.

KEY

ANCHOR STRANDED
COTTON (FLOSS)

　48　　　　　206

ANCHOR MARLITT

　813

ANCHOR PEARL
COTTON NO. 12

　48

FINISHED SIZE
8 x 8cm (3¼ x 3¼ in)

Reversed Faggot Filling

REVERSED FAGGOT FILLING is identical to the back of faggot filling but worked from the front. The open texture it produces contrasts well with denser stitches such as satin stitch and double cross stitch but it also combines well with open outline stitches, such as chain stitch or whipped back stitch, which is used to outline the wing of the dove in the design opposite.

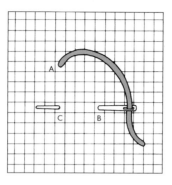

Fig 1. Bring the needle out at A, insert it at B, four threads down and four threads to the right, and bring it back out at C.

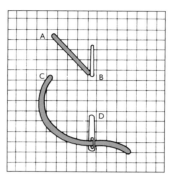

Fig 2. Insert the needle at D, four threads down and four threads to the right, and bring it out at B.

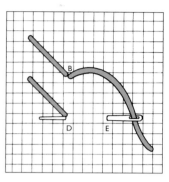

Fig 3. Insert the needle at E, four threads down and four threads to the right, and bring it out at D.

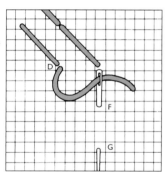

Fig 4. Insert the needle at F, four threads down and four threads to the right. To begin the next row bring the needle out at G. Turn the fabric upside down, ready to work the next row.

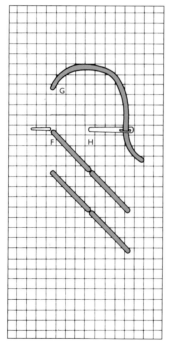

Fig 5. Insert the needle at H, four threads down and four threads to the right, and bring it out at F – you will be stitching back over the previous row.

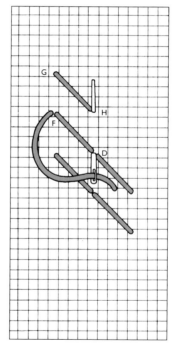

Fig 6. Re-insert the needle at D and bring it out at H. Continue in the same way.

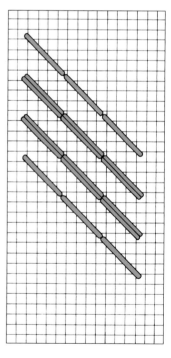

Fig 7. When you have completed an area the first and last rows of diagonal stitches will be worked singly; the centre rows will be worked twice.

Dove

This dove of peace design is worked in white on blue, as inspired by traditional china. A single strand of white Anchor Pearl Cotton No. 8 was used to outline the design in whipped back stitch (page 55) with No. 12 cotton used to work the wing in reversed faggot filling (opposite). Use No. 12 cotton to work the tail in fern stitch (page 57) and the eye as a small eyelet (page 32). For the additional straight stitches of the tail feathers use two strands of silver Coats Reflecta (301) and use the same thread to work the leaf sprig in the dove's beak in Holbein stitch (page 60) and chain stitch (page 56).

NOTE:
On this chart each square represents a block of 2 x 2 fabric threads.

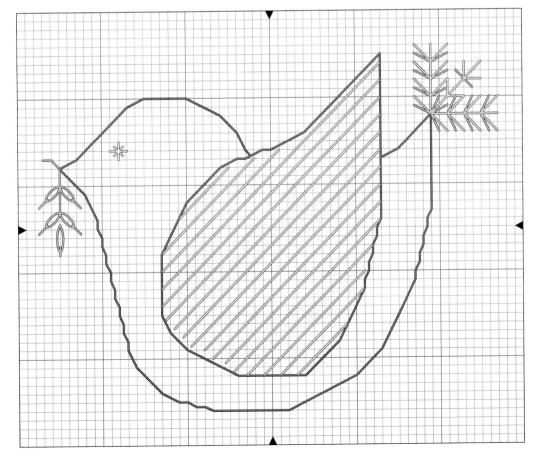

KEY

ANCHOR PEARL
COTTON

1 (No. 12)

1 (No. 8)

COATS REFLECTA

301

FINISHED SIZE
7 x 10cm (2¾ x 4in)

Four Sided Stitch

FOUR SIDED STITCH produces a close, fine, net-like effect that can look particularly delicate but is really very simple to work. It is similar in effect to double faggot filling except that each stitch is worked only once and a full square is completed at every stage. It is used to fill the Art Deco Rose, opposite.

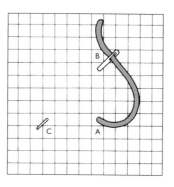

Fig 1. Bring the needle out at A, insert it at B, four threads up, and bring it out at C, four threads to the left of A, as shown.

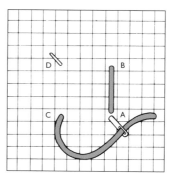

Fig 2. Insert the needle at A and bring it out at D, four threads above C.

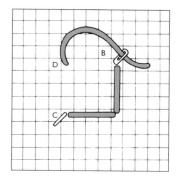

Fig 3. Insert the needle at B and bring it out at C again. Then complete the stitch by taking the needle back down at D.

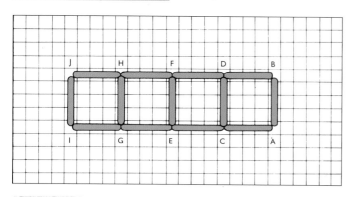

Fig 4. In a row of stitches the final stitch of the first square becomes the first stitch of the second square and so on. Work from right to left. When working subsequent rows, work back over the lower edge of the blocks above to create double horizontal lines in the same way as you create double vertical lines in the variation below.

Four Sided Stitch: Variation

THIS VARIATION of four sided stitch has staggered rows that pull the fabric threads into scallops. It exemplifies how with pulled thread work the art lies in the positioning of basic stitches rather than in the complicated manipulation of the threads. This stitch is used in the Wedding Sampler on page 52.

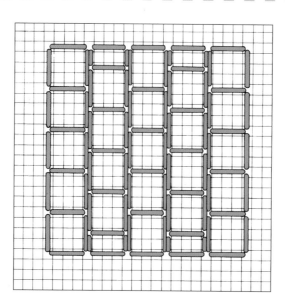

Work a row of four-sided stitch – in this case it is shown as a vertical row, but it can be worked horizontally. For the next row begin and end with a half stitch worked over 2 x 4 threads instead of the usual 4 x 4 threads. Work a standard row followed by another row with half stitches and each end and so on until the area is filled.

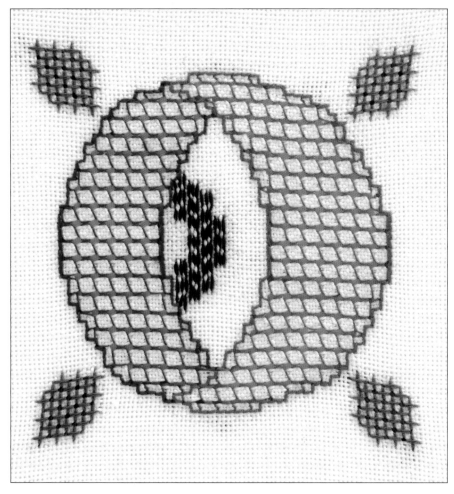

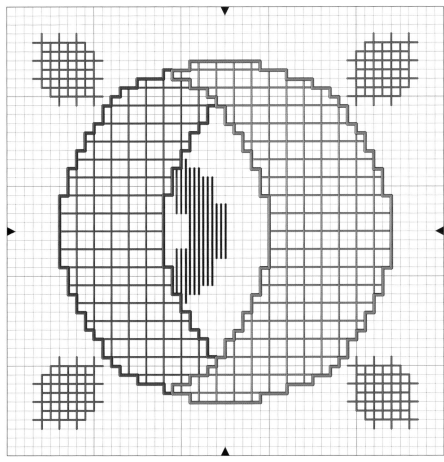

Art Deco Rose

Inspired by an Art Deco rose design, this stylized rose would suit many applications. Work on white Anchor Jobelan or the colour of your choice. Outline the rose in Holbein stitch (page 60), using two strands of 68 or 69 Anchor Stranded Cotton (floss). Fill the petals with four sided stitch (opposite), using the same colour as for the outline. Work the centre of the rose in 70 using Algerian filling stitch (page 22) and for the leaves use 877 in diagonal raised band filling (page 28).

NOTE:

On this chart each square represents a block of 2 x 2 fabric threads.

KEY

ANCHOR STRANDED
COTTON (FLOSS)

▦ 68	■ 70
▦ 69	▦ 877

FINISHED SIZE

8 x 8cm (3¼ x 3¼in)

Greek Cross Stitch: Lacy Filling

GREEK CROSS STITCH can be worked individually or in patterns as a filling stitch. Two commonly used patterns are lacy filling, shown here, and the squared variation, shown below. Lacy filling is used on the upper wings in the design shown opposite.

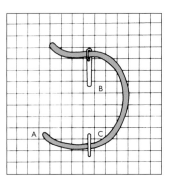

Fig 1. Bring the needle out at A, insert it at B, four threads up and four threads to the right, and bring it back out at C, keeping the thread under the needle, as shown.

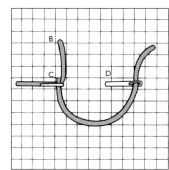

Fig 2. Pull the thread through and insert the needle at D, four threads to the right, bringing it out again at C and keeping the thread under the needle, as shown.

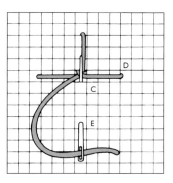

Fig 3. Pull the thread through and insert the needle at E, four threads down, bringing it out again at C, as shown.

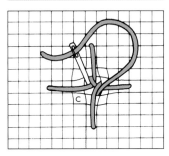

Fig 4. Pull the thread through and secure the cross by inserting the needle again at C, overlapping the last and first stitches.

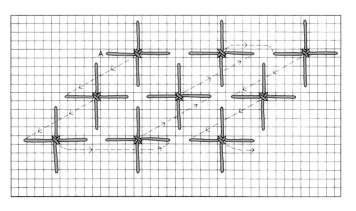

Fig 5. For lacy filling work each Greek cross over the same number of threads. Start the sequence at A. The broken lines indicate the direction of the connecting thread between stitches on the reverse side. Work diagonal rows.

Greek Cross Stitch: Squared Filling

THE SQUARED FILLING formation of Greek cross stitch is worked in diagonal rows, set so that the crosses form large squares. It is used in Frosted Fields (page 33) for the foreground field. Work each stitch over the same number of fabric threads.

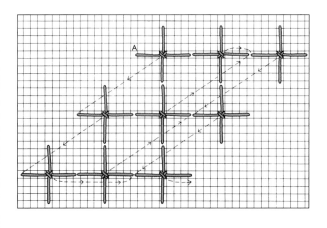

Following the diagram, begin the first stitch at A and work the crosses in diagonal rows. The broken lines indicate the direction of the connecting thread between stitches on the reverse side. On completion of the first diagonal row, turn the fabric and work the next diagonal row back beside the first. Work subsequent rows in the same way.

Dragonfly

To capture the translucency and iridescence of a dragonfly's wing, this design was stitched in two shades of glittering Coats Reflecta, with shimmering Anchor Marlitt for the body. Work the body in satin stitch (page 63) using two strands of blue Anchor Marlitt (835). For the upper wings use turquoise Coats Reflecta (316) and work in Greek cross stitch lacy filling (opposite). For the lower wings use 312 and work in cobbler filling (page 26). This dragonfly was stitched on white Anchor Jobelan so it would show up clearly, but it would also look lovely on denim blue or wood violet Anchor Jobelan or on light blue or mint green Anchor Evenweave fabric.

NOTE:
On this chart the gridlines represent individual fabric threads.

KEY

COATS REFLECTA

312

316

ANCHOR MARLITT

835

FINISHED SIZE
7 x 9.5cm (2¾ x 3¾in)

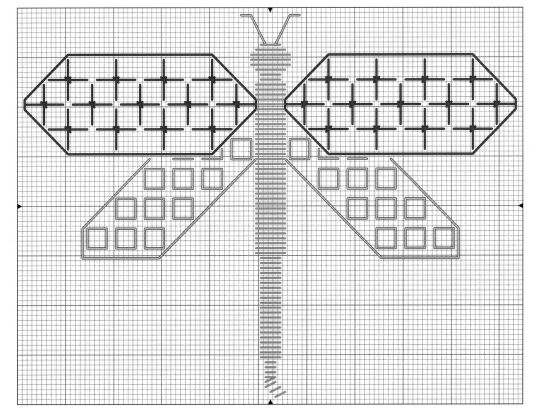

Honeycomb Filling

HONEYCOMB FILLING, as its name suggests, creates a honeycomb effect. This is more pronounced when the stitch is worked in a thread that will show up on the fabric, such as a darker shade. It is also useful for capturing the texture of seeds or flower heads, as in the design opposite.

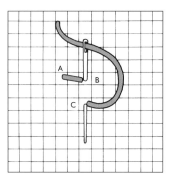

Fig 1. Bring the needle out at A, insert it at B, two threads to the right, and bring it out at C, two threads down. Insert the needle at B and bring it out at C again.

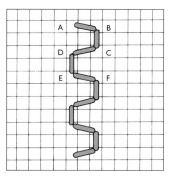

Fig 2. Continue as shown, going in at D, out at E, in at D again and back out at E, in at F and so on.

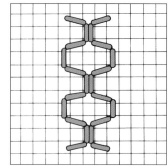

Fig 3. To work a second row position the stitches as shown, working the connecting stitches into the same holes. Repeat these two rows to fill an area.

Mosaic Filling

MOSAIC FILLING is perfect for geometrical designs in which its squared format comes into its own. It can be used individually or in blocks for borders as in the sampler on page 52. It is easier to work than it may appear, comprising satin stitch with four sided stitch and cross stitch.

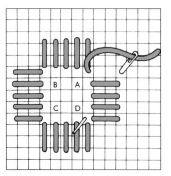

Fig 1. Starting at A, work five satin stitches (page 63) over three fabric threads to form a block. Bring the needle through again at B and work the next block. Work four blocks altogether to form a square. On completion of the last stitch, bring the needle through at D.

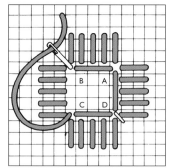

Fig 2. Work a four-sided stitch (see page 40) and on completion, bring the needle through again at D, as shown.

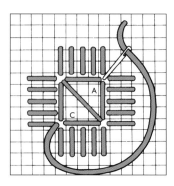

Fig 3. Stitch diagonally across the central square. Bring the needle out at C and insert it at A, as shown to complete the central cross stitch.

Sunflower

Honeycomb filling (opposite) captures the decorative seed head inside this sunflower, which is worked on co-ordinating coffee Anchor Jobelan fabric. Use a single strand of brown Anchor Marlitt (1140) for the honeycomb filling and then work the petals in fly stitch using two strands of orange/ brown Anchor Multicolor Stranded Cotton(1305). If desired, place one or more ladybirds anywhere in the design. The ladybird is worked in cross stitch (page 56) with each stitch worked over a single strand of the fabric thread in 46 and 403 cotton. Work the ladybird's spots as French knots (page 59).

NOTE:
On this chart the gridlines represent individual fabric threads except for the ladybird. Here each block represents one cross stitch worked over intersecting fabric threads.

KEY

ANCHOR STRANDED
COTTON (FLOSS)

46   1305 multicolor

403

ANCHOR MARLITT

1140

FINISHED SIZE
8 x 8cm (3¼ x 3¼in)

Outlined Diamond Eyelet Filling

OUTLINED DIAMOND EYELET FILLING is worked by stitching a diamond eyelet (page 32) surrounded by diagonal satin stitches. When worked in a contrast thread, this produces an ornate look reminiscent of Indian Shisha work and is ideal for describing the segmented skin of the pineapple in the design opposite.

Work the eyelets first, following the instructions on page 32, then work the outline in satin stitch in the same way as for mosaic filling (page 44). Here the eyelet is shown worked over 10 fabric threads, with the diagonal satin stitches worked over two intersections.

Punch Stitch

PUNCH STITCH is very similar to four-sided stitch (page 40) in effect but in this case the stitches are worked twice for greater impact and strength. It is used on the leaves of the blue hydrangea featured on page 31.

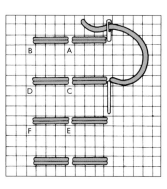

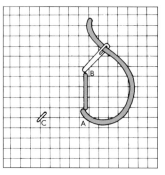

Fig 1. Bring the needle out at A, insert it at B, four threads up, and bring it out again at A; insert the needle again at B and bring it out at C, four threads down and four threads to the left.

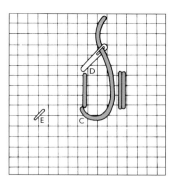

Fig 2. Insert the needle at D, four threads up, and bring it out again at C; insert the needle at D and bring it out at E. Continue working in this way for the required length.

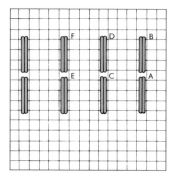

Fig 3. Turn the fabric to work the next row, as shown. Work all the rows required to fill the area.

Fig 4. To complete the squares, turn the fabric sideways and work the stitches as before.

Stitching Notes

Pineapple

Stitch this design over two threads of ivory Anchor Jobelan. Work the pineapple in outlined diamond eyelet filling (opposite) using two strands of Anchor Marlitt 848 and 1012. Work the leaves in fern stitch using two strands of Anchor Stranded Cotton in 241. Outline the border with running stitch using two strands of Anchor Marlitt 848, then fill the border using diamond eyelets in Anchor Stranded Cotton 300, leaf stitch variation (page 60) in 241 and the hearts in satin stitch (page 63) using 848.

NOTE:
On this chart the gridlines represent individual fabric threads.

KEY

ANCHOR STRANDED
COTTON (FLOSS)

■ 241

□ 300

ANCHOR MARLITT

■ 848

□ 1012

FINISHED SIZE
11 x 11cm (4¼ x 4¼ in)

Ripple Filling

RIPPLE FILLING is a configuration of double back stitch that creates an attractive ripple or wave effect when the threads are pulled tight. It is best to mount the fabric in a frame, especially when working over a large area to prevent distortions. Use a matching thread for subtle effects or a darker thread for greater impact, as in the Distant Sails design opposite.

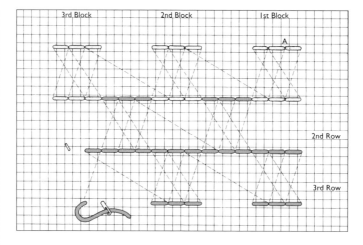

Begin the first block of the first row at A and work over the same number of fabric threads throughout, following the instructions for double back stitch on page 34. For an all-over filling work following the diagram. The broken lines indicate the thread on the reverse side. The grey stitches show the first row of blocks and the coloured stitches show subsequent blocks to make the diagram easier to follow.

Spaced Satin Filling

SPACED SATIN FILLING pulls the fabric into more distinct ripples or waves than ripple filling, above, this time by pulling the fabric into a series of spaced bars. The bars are arranged in a chequerboard pattern as in the foreground waves of the Distant Sails design opposite.

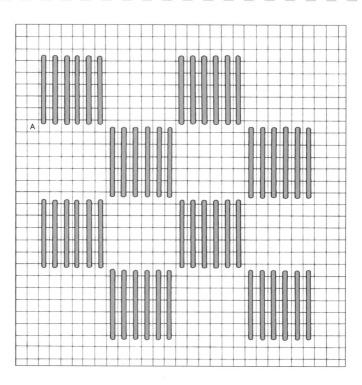

Beginning at A, work the first row of satin stitch blocks vertically or horizontally. (See page 63 for details on working satin stitch.) Work the second row of blocks so that they are positioned between the blocks of the first row. Continue working rows of blocks to fill the space.

Distant Sails

Spaced satin filling (opposite) is used here to suggest the waves in the foreground, worked with two strands of 940 at the front and 939 behind that. Ripple filling (page 48), worked in the lighter blue, creates the subtler waves in the distance. Florentine stitch (page 58), which is a formation of satin stitch, captures the density and colour of the sails. Use Anchor Marlitt 800 and 893 for the front sail and Anchor Stranded Cotton (floss) in 1 and 46 for the second sail. As a finishing touch, sea gulls roam the sky, worked in fly stitch (page 58) using white Anchor Stranded Cotton.

NOTE:
On this chart the gridlines represent individual fabric threads.

KEY

ANCHOR STRANDED
COTTON (FLOSS)

☐	1	☐	939
☐	46	☐	940

ANCHOR MARLITT

☐	893	☐	800

FINISHED SIZE
8 x 8cm (3¼ x 3¼in)

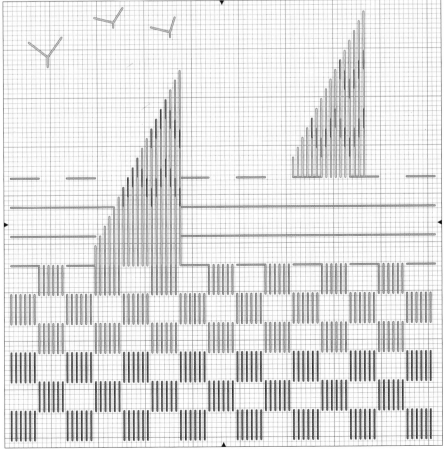

Step Filling

STEP FILLING is worked like spaced satin stitch except that blocks run in alternate directions, but this simple change gives this stitch a completely different look – that of a woven effect. It is used for the beehive in the design opposite.

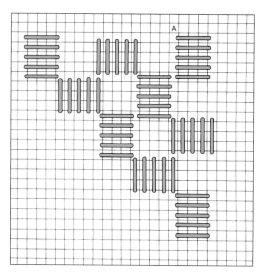

Beginning at A, work diagonal lines of satin stitch blocks (see page 63), with five stitches to a block and each block worked over four threads. Work one diagonal line with the satin stitches running horizontally, then work a diagonal line with the stitches running vertically and so on. All the stitches must be firmly pulled to achieve the desired effect.

Wave Stitch

WAVE STITCH is worked by stitching a series of connecting diagonal straight stitches that pull the fabric into a herringbone pattern of holes. When worked in a contrasting thread the diagonal lines of stitching become more prominent. It is used for a border in the Wedding Sampler on page 52.

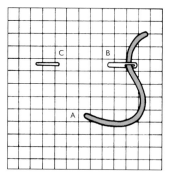

Fig 1. Bring the needle out at A, insert it at B, four threads up and two threads to the right, and bring it back out at C, four threads to the left.

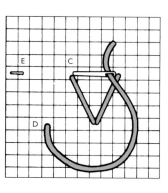

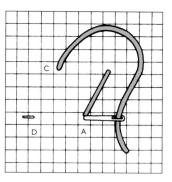

Fig 2. Insert the needle at A and bring it out at D, four threads to the left.

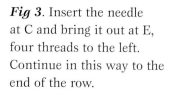

Fig 3. Insert the needle at C and bring it out at E, four threads to the left. Continue in this way to the end of the row.

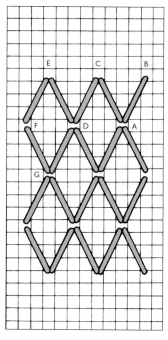

Fig 4. To work the second row, complete the stitch F to E and bring the needle out at G. Insert the needle at F, four threads up and two threads to the left, and bring it out at D. Continue as shown.

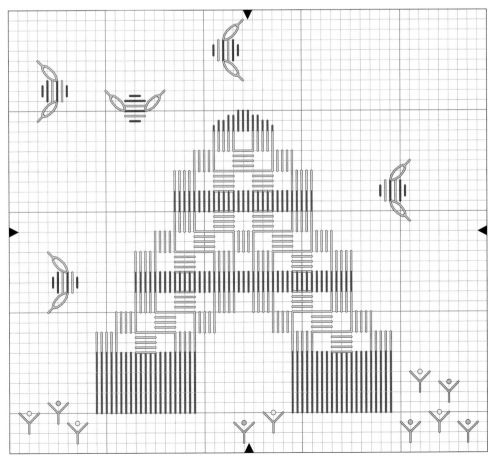

Stitching Notes

Beehive

Step filling (opposite) worked in Anchor Pearl Cotton No. 12 with bars of satin stitch (page 63) worked in No. 8 thread combine to create this towering beehive. The bees are worked in satin stitch using two strands of 305 and 360. Their wings are detached chain stitches (page 56) worked in Coats Reflecta (300). Work the leaves and stems of each flower as a fly stitch (page 58) using 253. Add French knot flowers in 108 and 48.

NOTE:
On this chart each square represents a block of 2 x 2 fabric threads.

KEY

ANCHOR STRANDED
COTTON (FLOSS)

▨	48	▨	305
▨	108	▨	360
▨	253		

ANCHOR PEARL COTTON

▨	387 (No.12)	▨	387 (No. 8)

COATS REFLECTA

▨ 300

FINISHED SIZE
7.5 x 9cm (3 x 3½in)

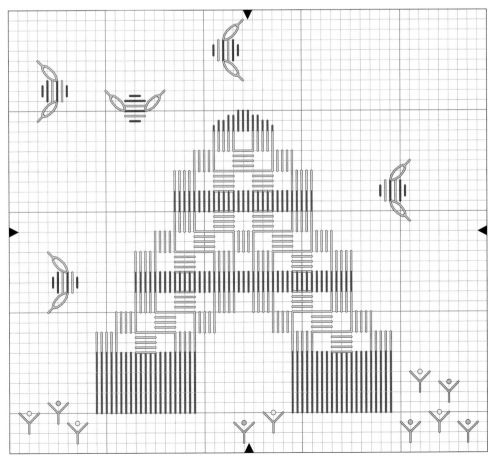

■ *This sampler could be adapted to celebrate any occasion, including the birth of a child, a special achievement or a wedding anniversary. To make it suitable for a girl's birth sampler, simply replace the blues 117 and 118 with pinks 75 and 76.*

Stitching Notes

Wedding Sampler

Outline the heart in Holbein stitch (page 60) in Coats Reflecta 301, then fill it in chequer filling (page 24) using Anchor Pearl Cotton No. 12 in white (1). Work the flowers beneath in cross stitch (page 56) using two strands of cotton (floss) in 117 and 118, and work the leaves in 1042. Work the name(s) in back stitch (page 55), using 118 and referring to the alphabet chart and instructions on page 54. Under the name work a band of rice stitch (page 63) using white Anchor Marlitt and silver Coats Reflecta followed by a line of cable stitch (page 55) in Anchor Pearl Cotton No 12. Below this work a line of diamond filling (page 32) in Anchor Pearl Cotton No. 12 with a heart worked in satin stitch (page 63) inside every diamond. Work two rows of mosaic filling (page 44) then work the date, as for the name. Now work a band of three overlapping rows of long-armed cross stitch (page 61) with a band of four sided stitch variation (page 40) beneath it in Anchor Pearl Cotton. Use Anchor Marlitt to work individual Rhodes stitches (page 62) with a cross stitch in Coats Reflecta between each one and then work a row of wave stitch (page 50) beneath this in Anchor Pearl Cotton. Finally, work further flowers and leaves in cross stitch as before.

KEY

ANCHOR STRANDED
COTTON (FLOSS)

 117   118

1042

ANCHOR MARLITT

800

COATS REFLECTA

301

ANCHOR PEARL COTTON

1 (No. 12)

FINISHED SIZE
18 x 9.5cm (7 x 3¾in)

NOTE:
*On this chart each
square represents a block
of 2 x 2 fabric threads.*

Alphabet Chart

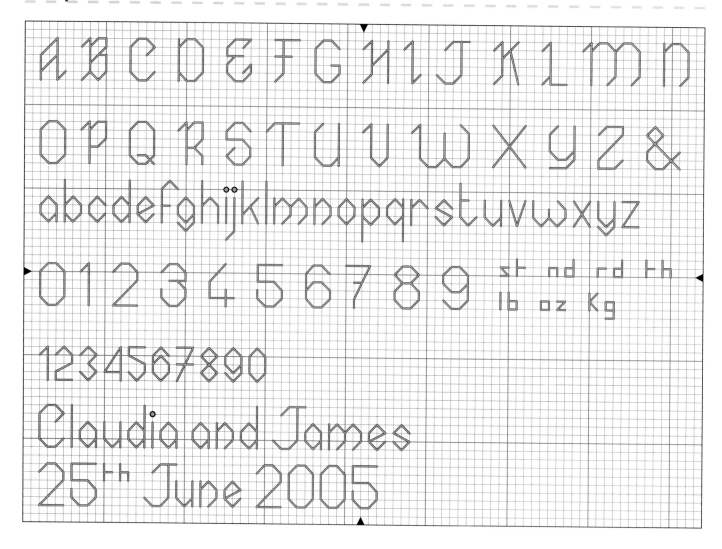

Personalizing Your Sampler

Adding your own names and dates to the sampler requires a bit of charting, which is much easier than it sounds. First you need to know the size of the area you have to work on. The sampler is worked over a width of 53 blocks of 2 x 2 fabric threads with one block unstitched at each side.

Now you need to see how much space your words and numbers require. On a piece of graph paper, plot the letters you need from the alphabet chart above, leaving one block between letters and two blocks between words. Count the number of blocks required and deduct this from the width you have to work on – in this case 53. Divide the result by two to find the number of blocks you should leave blank at each end of the stitching. If you have an uneven number, add an extra block space between two of the words, or reduce the spacing between the words slightly

If the words require more space than you have in the design, you will need to work them on two lines. In this case omit one of the decorative bands and plot the words as before, centred over two lines each five blocks high with at least two blocks between the lines.

■ *Use the chart above to personalize the Wedding Sampler on the previous page or to add wording to any of the designs in this book.*

Complementary Stitches

The following 18 stitches will enable you to add structure and detail to pulled thread work.

Back Stitch: Whipped

WHIPPED BACK STITCH is a useful outline stitch that can be worked in one or two colours. It is thicker than ordinary back stitch and produces a slightly wavy line that will add variety to your work. This stitch is used to outline the strawberry in the design on page 27.

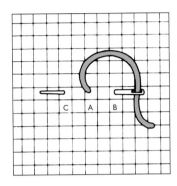 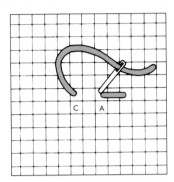 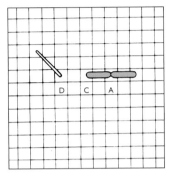

Fig 1. Bring the needle out at A, insert it at B, two threads to the right, and bring it back out at C, four threads to the left.

Fig 2. Insert the needle at A, two threads to the right.

Fig 3. Bring the needle out four threads to the left at D. Continue in this way to work a line of back stitch.

Fig 4. Using the same or a contrasting thread, bring the needle out at B and pass it under each stitch in turn without piercing the fabric. Take the thread to the back to finish.

Cable Stitch

CABLE STITCH produces a double outline and may or may not be worked as a pulled stitch. It can be worked over any even number of fabric threads. When turning a corner, the outer stitches will need to be worked over one less stitch to maintain the rhythm of the stitch. This bold outline stitch is used in the Wedding Sampler (page 52).

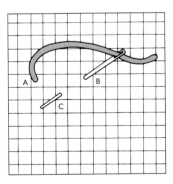 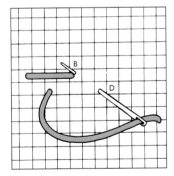 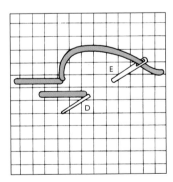

Fig 1. Bring the needle out at A and insert it at B, four threads to the right, bringing it back out at C, one thread down and two threads to the left.

Fig 2. Insert the needle at D, four threads to the right, and bring it out at B, one thread up and two threads to the left.

Fig 3. Continue the process, inserting the needle at E and bringing it back out at D and so on.

Chain Stitch

CHAIN STITCH is a popular outline stitch that may also be worked as a filling, when it emulates the appearance of knitting. It can be worked over any number of fabric threads. In the Beehive design on page 51 it is used in its detached (individual) form for the bees' wings.

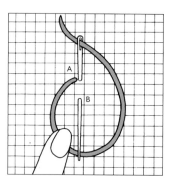

Fig 1. Bring the needle out at A, hold the thread down with your thumb, and re-insert the needle at A, bringing it up at B, the required number of fabric threads away. Keep the thread under the needle.

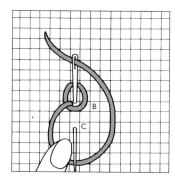

Fig 2. Pull the thread through gently but firmly and repeat the process to work the next and subsequent stitches. Secure the final chain by taking a small stitch over the end.

Cross Stitch

CROSS STITCH is one of the simplest and best-loved stitches the world over. It is usually worked over a block of 2 x 2 fabric threads but it can also be worked over one intersection of threads when it is known as petite cross, or over a larger block, if desired. It is used in the Wedding Sampler (page 52).

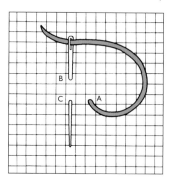

Fig 1. Bring the needle out at A, insert it at B, two threads up and two threads to the left, and bring it back out two threads below at C.

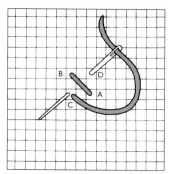

Fig 2. Insert the needle at D and bring it out at C ready to work the next cross stitch.

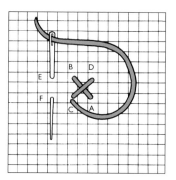

Fig 3. Work the next and subsequent stitches in the same way. Alternatively, work a series of half cross stitches, A–B, C–E and so on along the full line, then work the second part of each cross stitch on the return journey.

■ *Perfect Stitching*
For a neat result when using cross stitch make sure that all of your top stitches lie in the same direction.

Double Cross Stitch

DOUBLE CROSS STITCH is a decorative variation of cross stitch produced by adding a vertical and horizontal stitch over a cross stitch. It is worked over an even number of fabric threads, usually a block of 2 x 2 or 4 x 4 fabric threads. It is used to outline the petals in Cherry Blossom (page 37).

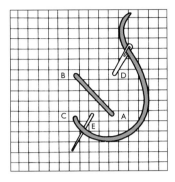

Fig 1. Start by working a cross stitch in the usual way as follows. Bring the needle out at A, insert it at B, four threads up and four threads to the left, and bring it back out four threads below at C. Complete the cross stitch by inserting the needle at D, then bring it out at E.

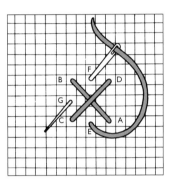

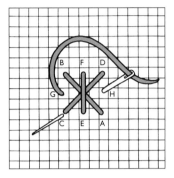

Fig 2. Insert the needle at F, between B and D, and bring it back out at G, between B and C.

Fig 3. Insert the needle at H to finish the double cross stitch and bring the needle out a C, ready to work the next stitch.

Fern Stitch

FERN STITCH is worked in simple straight stitches and produces a lovely feathery effect that is ideal for suggesting foliage or feathers as on the tail of the dove featured on page 39. This surface embroidery stitch combines well with pulled work.

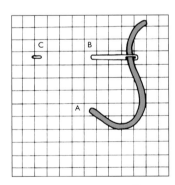

Fig 1. Bring the needle out at A, insert it at B and bring it out again at C.

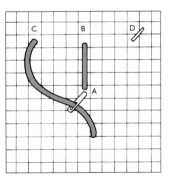

Fig 2. Insert the needle again at A and bring it out at D.

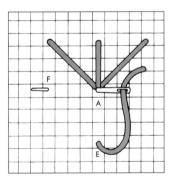

Fig 3. Insert the needle again at A and bring it out at E, then insert it again at A and bring it out at F. Continue working in sequence.

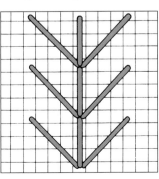

Fig 4. This shows the finished effect of the stitch.

Florentine Stitch

FLORENTINE STITCH is created by working straight stitches in staggered formation and is the foundation of Bargello work. Being based on a pattern of straight stitches it complements pulled work beautifully. It is used on the sails of the ships in Distant Sails on page 49.

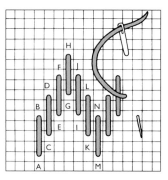

Fig 1. Bring the needle out at A and insert it at B, four or six fabric threads up. Bring the needle out at C, halfway between A and B and one thread to the right, and insert it at D, four or six fabric threads up. Work in an up and down sequence as shown.

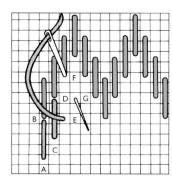

Fig 2. Work the next line of stitching immediately below the first, as shown.

Fly Stitch

FLY STITCH consists of a loop held down by a vertical stitch. The proportions of the stitch can be varied so that it resembles a 'V' or a 'Y' and it can be worked over any number of threads as an outline or individual stitch, producing different decorative effects. In Festive Lace (page 29) it is worked in a line for a leafy effect.

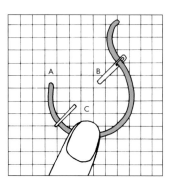

Fig 1. Bring the needle out at A. Hold the thread down with the thumb and insert the needle at B, an even number of threads to the right, bringing it out at C, exactly between A and B and a little way down, as shown.

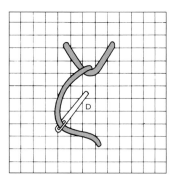

Fig 2. Insert the needle at D, below C, to complete the fly stitch.

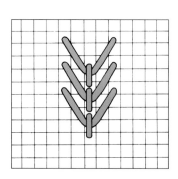

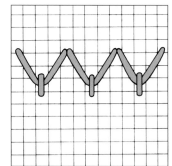

Fig 3. This stitch can be worked in horizontal rows, creating a zigzag effect.

Fig 4. Alternatively, set the stitch in vertical rows, as shown here.

French Knot

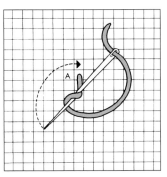

FRENCH KNOTS are small, decorative knots worked on the right side of the fabric. These are ideal for describing small details, such as birds' eyes, or they can be worked together as a highly textured filling. In Festive Lace (page 29) they are used to suggest berries in the decorative border.

Fig 1. Bring the needle out at A, at the knot position. Twist the thread once or twice around the needle, depending on the size of knot required.

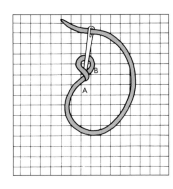

Fig 2. Holding the knot in place, insert the needle one fabric thread away and pull the thread through. Secure the knot on the wrong side by taking a small catching stitch under nearby embroidery threads.

Hemstitch

HEMSTITCH adds an attractive border to any counted thread work that will be finished with a hem and is used for the place mat shown on page 18. There are a number of different variations produced by altering the position of the stitches or by adding new ones. The variation shown here is ladder hemstitch.

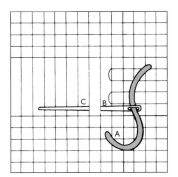

Fig 1. Withdraw the required number of cross threads by snipping and darning the ends back in. Now bring the needle out at A and pass it from B to C behind two loose vertical threads.

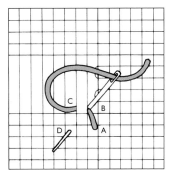

Fig 2. Pull the thread through, insert the needle at B and bring it out at D, below C and level with A.

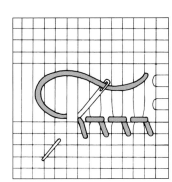

Fig 3. Continue working in the same way along the full length, as shown.

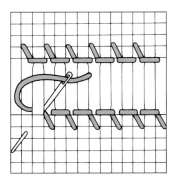

Fig 4. For ladder hemstitch turn the fabric and work hemstitch along the opposite side of the withdrawn threads, taking the needle under the same pairs of threads as before.

Holbein Stitch

HOLBEIN STITCH is also known as double running stitch and is one of the easiest and most satisfying of the outline stitches. All you do is work evenly spaced running stitch and fill in the gaps on the return journey. It looks the same from both sides and therefore was traditionally used to decorate collars and other items that might be viewed from behind. It features in Grapes (page 23) where it is used to work the tendrils.

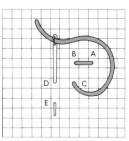

Fig 1. Bring the needle out at A, at the start of the line. Insert the needle at B and bring it out at C. Insert the needle at D and bring it out at E. Continue in the same way.

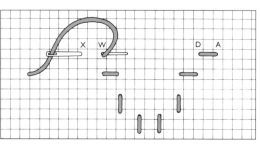

Fig 2. When you reach the end of the design line bring the needle back out at the start of the final stitch, as shown.

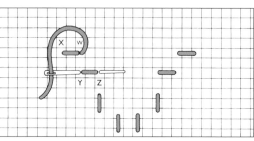

Fig 3. Continue back along the line, filling in the spaces between the existing stitches. Your design line can be straight or twist and turn as much as desired.

Leaf Stitch Variation

LEAF STITCH VARIATION, as its name suggests, looks like a leaf, but you don't have to use it purely for this purpose; set in staggered horizontal lines, this stitch makes an attractive filling stitch or a textured border design. It is used in the Strawberry design (page 27) for the strawberry leaves and again in the decorative border.

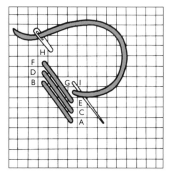

Fig 1. Bring the needle out at A, at the base of the leaf. Insert it at B and bring it out at C. Work two more parallel stitches, as shown, then begin to shape the leaf by inserting the needle at H and bringing it out at I.

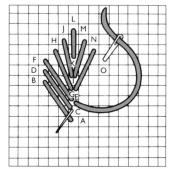

Fig 2. Work up to the top of the leaf, then come down the other side, exactly reflecting the first side and working the stitches on the second side into the same centre holes as the stitches on the first side.

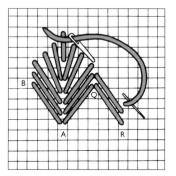

Fig 3. When working leaf stitch variation as a filling, position the second leaf as shown. On the next line the top of a leaf will be at B and then again at Q.

Long-Armed Cross Stitch

LONG-ARMED CROSS STITCH is also known as plaited Slav and Portuguese twist. In diagram form it looks like a wonky cross stitch, but when worked in thread it looks like fine braid and makes an excellent outline stitch. In Flower Basket (page 25) it is used to fill the basket handle.

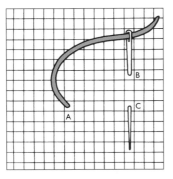

Fig 1. Working from left to right, bring the needle out at A and insert it at B, bringing it back out at C. Here B is shown six threads across and three threads up, but you could position it four threads over and two up or two threads over and one up.

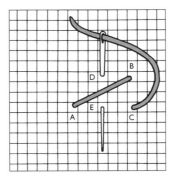

Fig 2. Insert the needle level with B and halfway between A and B. Bring it back out at E, centred between A and C, ready to work the next stitch.

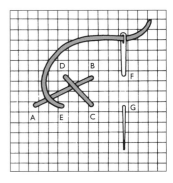

Fig 3. Continue in the same way, working a series of uneven crosses. (The next stitch will go in at B and come out at C.)

Milanese Pinwheel

MILANESE PINWHEEL is a configuration of Milanese stitch, a simple triangle of satin stitch that can be arranged in all sorts of ways to create an attractive filling. Milanese stitch is shown in figure 1 and the pinwheel configuration is explained in figures 2 and 3. Milanese pinwheels are used in the Flower Basket design on page 25.

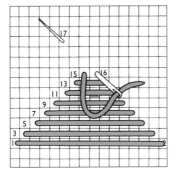

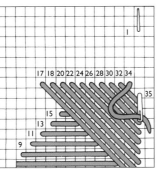

Fig 1. Starting with the longest stitch, work a series of satin stitches in a triangle with each stitch progressively smaller than the last. This is Milanese stitch. Here the largest stitch is worked over fifteen threads, but it can be worked over any uneven number of threads from seven upwards (four along the side edge).

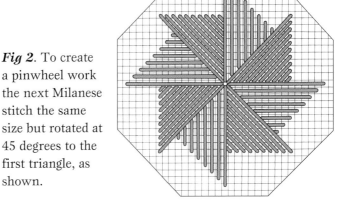

Fig 2. To create a pinwheel work the next Milanese stitch the same size but rotated at 45 degrees to the first triangle, as shown.

Fig 3. Continue in the same way, working a total of eight triangles to complete the pinwheel.

Octagonal Rhodes Stitch

OCTAGONAL RHODES STITCH is a variation of Rhodes stitch (below) that can be used on its own as in Flower Basket (page 25) or positioned in rows with Rhodes stitch set diagonally in the gaps to create a dense filling. This stitch can be worked any size, with three or more stitches to each edge.

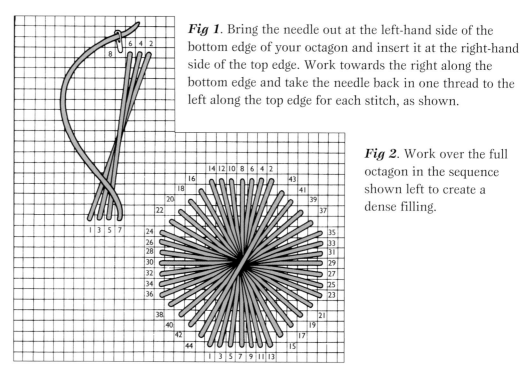

Fig 1. Bring the needle out at the left-hand side of the bottom edge of your octagon and insert it at the right-hand side of the top edge. Work towards the right along the bottom edge and take the needle back in one thread to the left along the top edge for each stitch, as shown.

Fig 2. Work over the full octagon in the sequence shown left to create a dense filling.

Rhodes Stitch

RHODES STITCH is named after Mary Rhodes, the English needlework designer who created it. It is a chunky square filling that can be worked over an area of three by three fabric threads or more, but which looks best when worked over five or more threads, as shown here. In the Wedding Sampler on page 52 it is used for one of the bands.

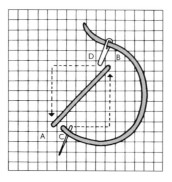

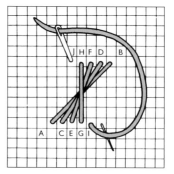

Fig 1. Bring the needle out at A, at the bottom-left corner of the square, and insert it at the top-right corner at B. Bring it out at C, one thread to the right of A, and insert it at D, one thread to the left of B.

Fig 2. Continue round the square in the same way, as shown.

Fig 3. If desired, you can work a small straight stitch at the centre of the square to hold down the threads, as shown.

Rice Stitch

RICE STITCH is a traditional stitch based on a cross stitch worked over an even number of fabric threads. It creates an attractive latticework effect that complements the lacy effect of many pulled thread stitches, and it can be worked in one or two colours. It is used in the Wedding Sampler on page 52.

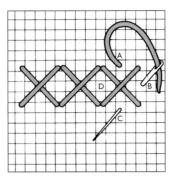

Fig 1. Work a line of cross stitches (page 56) over an even number of fabric threads. Here each stitch is worked over a block of 4 x 4 fabric threads. Using the same or a different colour of thread, bring the needle out at the centre top of the first cross, at A, pass it in at the side, at B, and bring it back out at the bottom, at C, as shown.

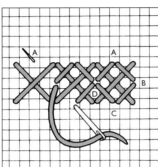

Fig 2. Take the needle back in at B, bringing it out at D and then pass it in at A and back out at D. Take it in at C to complete the first set of small crosses. To work the next set of crosses, bring the needle out at the top of the next cross stitch, at A and repeat the sequence.

Satin Stitch

SATIN STITCH is the stalwart of many embroidery designs and no stitching repertoire would be complete without it. It is used for the body in the Dragonfly design on page 43 and in more stylized form in the Beehive design on page 51.

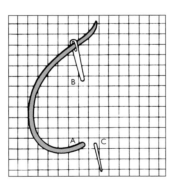

Fig 1. For vertical satin stitch, bring the needle out at A at the base of the shape and insert it at B at the top of the shape, bringing it back out at C, next to A.

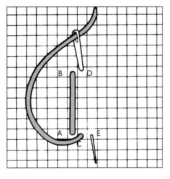

Fig 2. Continue to work parallel stitches, as shown, adjusting their length to fill the desired shape.

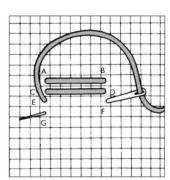

Fig 3. Satin stitch can be worked in any direction, even diagonally. The direction of stitches has a major impact on the effect of the stitch and how it reflects the light, so always think about which way to work it before you begin.

Suppliers

UK
Coats Crafts UK
PO Box 22, Lingfield House, Lingfield Point,
McMullen Road, Darlington Co. Durham DL1 1YQ
Tel: + 1 325 394237 (consumer helpline)
Fax: + 1 325 394200
www.coatscrafts.co.uk

USA
Coats and Clark
PO Box 12229
Greenville
SC29612 – 0229
Tel: (800) 648 1479
www.coatsandclark.com

Index